State policies and the position of
women workers in the People's Democratic
Republic of Yemen, 1967-77

Women, Work and Development, 3

State policies and the position of women workers in the People's Democratic Republic of Yemen, 1967-77

Maxine Molyneux

Published with the financial support of the
United Nations Fund for Population Activities
(UNFPA)

International Labour Office   Geneva

ISBN 92-2-103144-6
ISSN 0253-2042

First published 1982
Second impression 1984

Printed in Switzerland

PREFACE

Since achieving independence from the United Kingdom in 1967, the Government of the Democratic Republic of Yemen set in train a series of radical transformations of the economy and society which have profoundly influenced the position of women. As part of its programme the revolutionary government has made an express commitment to establish formal equality between the sexes in all areas of social life. A series of major legal and educational reforms have been promulgated and many women have been mobilised for the first time into political and economic activity.

This experience in mobilising women is of interest for two main reasons. First, as a result of these reforms, Democratic Yemen can be ranked among the most radical of governments in the region in the realm of policy on women and is an example of what can be achieved by a state committed to granting women equal rights and opportunities. An account and assessment of the experience of Democratic Yemen in implementing these policies will therefore enable some comparison to be made with other countries, whether these be of a more traditional or radical orientation.

The second reason why Democratic Yemen is of special interest is that while it is a Muslim country it is also one influenced by socialist doctrine. Our knowledge of how the combination of Islam and socialism affects the position of women has until now been confined to the Muslim areas of the USSR. Little research has been carried out on the Muslim populations in other socialist states.

For these two reasons, Democratic Yemen constitutes a valuable case study, and this book will attempt to document and evaluate the main changes in the position of women that have occurred since Democratic Yemen gained Independence in 1967. It is based both upon fieldwork and upon the analysis of the available secondary sources. The discussion falls into two main parts corresponding to different but related objects of analysis. The first is concerned with government policies aimed at improving the position of women and it analyses their theoretical basis and their practical effects in four specific areas: juridical reform, political participation, education and employment. Part II will attempt to cast light on the position of those women who have been mobilised into economic activity. By analysing the home and work conditions of 120 female factory workers, the more diffuse effects of government policies, as well as their limitations, are thrown more sharply into focus. At the same time the information presented on these women workers contributes to our understanding of the character and composition of the female industrial proletariat in Third World countries. The women considered here are all the more interesting for being Democratic Yemen's first generation of female workers employed in the modern industrial sector.

Interesting though Democratic Yemen is, little sociological research has yet been undertaken there, and even less on women. Few independent research projects have been carried out, and even for these the problems of data collection have been considerable. Consequently the secondary sources are limited both in number and,

v

with some notable exceptions, in scope and quality. This is especially true of the statistical material since at the time of writing the government has not yet published the full results of the 1973 Census. The other statistical information that is available is incomplete, and in some cases either inconsistent or unreliable. It must therefore be borne in mind that the figures included in this report are only approximations, and the conclusions reached necessarily tentative.

Because of the limited source material available, this study has had to rely to a considerable extent more than is usual on primary material — in this case the results of over 170 interviews with individuals that were conducted during a research visit to Democratic Yemen at the end of 1977. Most of these were carried out in Aden, although a substantial minority were conducted in the Second, Third and Fifth Governorates. The informants included men and women with a wide range of experience — peasants, workers, ministers, administrators, journalists, planners, housewives, political activists, writers, historians, nurses and students, to name but a few. By far the largest number of interviews, 120 in all, were with women working in factories in Aden, and it is the findings from these interviews which comprise Part II of this study.

I would like to thank the ILO, the Government of the People's Democratic Republic of Yemen and the Fuller Bequest of the Sociology Department at the University of Essex, for their help in realising this research. In addition, I should like to thank those who have helped at various stages in this project, especially Richard Anker at the ILO, Fred Halliday, Lisa Croll and Holly Sutherland. Thanks too to Phil Holden and Carol O'Day for their computer work, and to Linda George for her work on the typescript.

Maxine Molynex
University of Essex

TABLE OF CONTENTS

INTRODUCTION

As the literature on the People's Democratic Republic of Yemen is limited, it may be helpful to set this book in context by giving a brief account of the country's socio-economic structure. Democratic Yemen occupies the south-western corner of the Arabian Peninsula and is bordered by the Yemen Arab Republic to the north, by Saudi Arabia to the north-east and by Oman to the east. It covers an area of 112,000 square miles and has a population of only 1.9 million (1979), 10 per cent of whom are nomads. The capital is Aden, on the Red Sea coast, historically the country's main centre of economic activity with its large deep-water harbour. With the exception of the fertile valleys of the Hadramaut region, the hinterland consists mainly of barren rock and desert. Rainfall is less than 3 inches on average a year and although the majority of the population live by subsistence farming and petty commodity production, only 2 per cent of the total land surface is cultivated. Democratic Yemen has few natural resources and, until the discovery of some oil and gold in 1980, no known mineral reserves of any significance. Apart from its income from the port, it relies on fishing and remittances from its 300,000 or more emigrants in the oil-producing states to earn much of its foreign exchange (World Bank, 1979). With an income per capita of only $480 per annum in 1979 it is one of the poorest countries in the world (World Bank, 1981).

The United Kingdom had ruled Aden as a colony since 1839 and had by the 1930s gradually extended control over the hinterland mini-states to encompass the area now known as Democratic Yemen. The last two decades of colonial rule were marked by an attempt to forge a Federation out of Aden and the 23 states of the interior. It was the defeat of this project and of a rival guerilla grouping, FLOSY, in a guerilla struggle that lasted for four years from its inception in 1963 which brought the revolutionary National Liberation Front to power in November 1967.[1] The Front (renamed the Yemeni Socialist Party in 1978) has governed the country since Independence and has applied its development policies in accordance with its socialist orientation. During the 1970s Democratic Yemen became increasingly reliant on the USSR and Eastern Europe for military and economic aid and at the same time came to adopt a number of political and social policies which bear the influence of this alliance.

Prior to the seizure of power by the revolutionary forces, Democratic Yemen suffered from the familiar catalogue of problems associated with extreme poverty and underdevelopment. In the first place, it had a weak productive structure in both agriculture and industry. Despite the importance of the agricultural sector to the economy, productivity remained low. The production of basic necessities was not developed to meet local demand and imports of food products were consequently high. The only substantial export crop was provided by two cotton projects established by the colonial government. In the capital, Aden, economic activity was primarily geared to servicing the port, the colonial administrative apparatus, and the military base. Although industry contributed 6.5 per cent of GNP, 3.5 per cent of this was accounted for by the oil refinery servicing the port. There was little local industry of any kind

1

beyond small artisanal workshops and manufacturing plants which employed around 5,000 workers. On the other hand, there developed a substantial service sector and a buoyant commercial sector trading in imported goods. However, the economy was severely affected by the closure of the Suez Canal in 1967 which together with the removal of the British military base, resulted in the loss of an estimated 15,000 jobs. At the same time the commercial sector contracted and remained depressed until the economic revival which began in 1973 (see Democratic Yemen, Ministry of Economy, Commerce and Planning, 1968).

The second problem facing the new government was that basic welfare provisions and educational opportunities were unavailable to all but a small minority of the population and were almost non-existent outside Aden. Under 400 schools and around 70 doctors catered to the country's more fortunate citizens and left the rest of the population to folk remedies and in the hands of religious educators (Democratic Yemen, Ministry of Economy, Commerce and Planning, 1968). This meant that, if the government was to realise its aim of providing free health care and educational facilities, it would have to divert a substantial percentage of its resources to doing so at the risk of starving the economy of necessary inputs.

Thirdly, Democratic Yemen lacked a unified national economy and a unified political structure. The inland area was not only constitutionally separate from Aden but was itself politically and economically fragmented as a result of sheikhs, sultans and emirs having retained considerable local autonomy. The area outside Aden was characterised by a marked division between town and country, and by a preponderance of pre-capitalist relations of production, diverse in form and ranging from the nomadic pastoralism characteristic of the Bedouin tribes to the more diversified class structure typical of the towns. Some areas such as the Hadramaut were characterised by a many-tiered caste system, which had survived despite decades of migration, increasing commercialism, and social differentiation in some of the wealthier inland areas.[2]

1. Women's place in pre-revolutionary society

The position of women within this poor and highly differentiated country was subject to class and regional variations within the limits imposed by local customs and religious practices. These variations included the degree to which seclusion, segregation and veiling were practiced and whether bride price or dowry systems, or both, prevailed. The existing differentials were exacerbated by the development of trade and commodity production in some areas, and in Aden, by the effects of urban development and contact with the international market.

On the eve of Independence the following picture of the differential position of women emerges. In Aden the situation had by the late 1950s begun to change for certain classes of women. The rules of seclusion were slowly becoming more relaxed, although the veil and *sheidor*[3] were worn by all but the women at the two extremes of the social structure — the handful of educated women and the very poor. The former, from some of the wealthier families, were sometimes sent abroad to Beirut or Cairo to study and on their return took up work in those occupations which were beginning to open up for women, such as education and the medical profession (see Ingrams,

2

1970). For the average women in the city there were far fewer opportunities, as areas of employment typically occupied by women in other developing countries, such as domestic work, clerical work and manufacturing, remained dominated by men and boys, most of them migrants from the interior, or the Yemen Arab Republic. One exception to this general rule was a specific category of women who were unveiled and did various forms of manual labour. These were migrant women, who, desperate for an income and freed from the restrictions of (and deprived of the status of) seclusion,[4] formed a stratum of low paid workers engaged primarily in such activities as sweeping streets and factory floors, in effect doing work that was considered too debased for Yemenis whether women or men. These women were either Somalis or members of a caste called the *akhdam* (literally "servants") allegedly descended from slaves. Both groups lived on the margin of society, generally in the shanties of Aden town.

In the countryside there operated the familiar disjuncture between social status and economic activity. Women were almost totally excluded from positions of social influence which were generally in the hands of elder males. But women played a major role in agriculture, and in many parts of rural Democratic Yemen were unveiled, although restrictions and segregation still operated. The division of labour was based on sex and this allocated to women the full range of domestic responsibilities including such activities as gathering firewood and carrying water. Women also tended animals and participated in certain agricultural tasks such as sowing and harvesting.[5] Indeed, since men took the afternoon off to sit together chewing the local narcotic *qat*, an activity from which women were excluded, women's contribution in some areas to agricultural production was probably greater than men's. This was especially true of regions affected by large-scale male out-migration. This pattern of social marginalisation and economic centrality is, of course, that found in many peasant societies.[6]

Despite these regional and class variations, women shared a common secondary status to men in the law and social life, and enjoyed fewer rights than men in marriage. Virtually all the population are Sunni Muslims of the Shafei variety and as in many Muslim societies women and men led segregated lives articulated upon a clearly defined sexual division of labour and gender hierarchy in which women were both separate, and inferior in status. Whereas the public domain, the world of social responsibility and authority, belonged to men, women's domain was in the home, and even there, the authority that individual women exercised was contingent on their age and status within the female hierarchy. A young wife could be made the virtual servant of her mother-in-law, or in polygamous households, of the senior wives. In general, however, a women's status in the family and in society at large was directly bound up with her ability to produce male heirs; apart from the idea that it was humiliating to beget daughters, the failure to produce sons was often sufficient reason for a divorce, even after a relatively short period of time.[7]

The strict controls exercised over women meant that their independent initiatives were closely circumscribed. At the onset of puberty or even before, they were forbidden to have any social contact with men not covered by the incest taboo.[8] A high premium was placed on virginity before marriage and on female sexual fidelity within marriage. The penalties for infringing such rules, or for being thought to do so, ranged from beating to death at the hands of husbands or relatives avenging the loss of honour (*Ird*) which such actions were thought to incur.[9] At the same time men's sexual freedom was less circumscribed; men were permitted polygamous marriages and until

3

the 1950s, concubines, and the existence in the pre-revolutionary period of open prostitution in Aden and Mukalla, the port towns of Democratic Yemen, attests to the absence of strong legal or social disincentives against it.

2. Socialist policies

After the government came to power in 1967, it began to implement a set of policies designed to tackle the problems of economic and social development, and in so doing to alter the position of women. In this sense developmental goals coincided with social policies designed to emancipate previously oppressed groups and classes from the constraints of the old order. These transformations followed the pattern found in most socialist countries (for a comparative overview see Molyneux, 1981).

Socialist states are generally committed to the view that what they term "traditional" or "feudal" residues constitute obstacles to economic development and social reform. The old order must therefore be dismantled and progressively replaced by a new centralised, secular and more egalitarian society more suited to the demands of economic development. In most socialist countries, particularly those of the Third World, this has involved an attempt to bring about a comparatively rapid transformation of the pre-revolutionary order in the process of which its social relations, ideologies, legal, political and religious systems are reformed or dismantled. This erosion or transformation of the old order has profound implications for the position of women, since it involves attacking some of the social relations and institutions within which their subordination is inscribed. This is especially the case in Third World countries where the weight of customary practices tends to bear heavily on women. Yet institutions such as polygamy, brideprice, child marriages and seclusion are also woven into the very fabric of pre-capitalist formations and some of these practices may be necessary for the survival of the old order. Without endorsing a reductionist or oversimplified account of these phenomena, it can still be recognised that systems of inheritance which discriminate against women, and the strict control of marriage alliances by kin groups may be central means by which forms of pre-capitalist property and social relations are maintained. Thus, the dismantling of structures that form an integral part of the pre-capitalist order can significantly improve the position of women; conversely, improving the position of women is seen by reforming governments as a key to dismantling the pre-capitalist social structure.

This coincidence of developmental goals and the freeing of women from the more archaic forms of subordination is often explicitly acknowledged in the literature of socialist states; discrimination against women is deplored not just on moral grounds but on the grounds that it is the result of "feudal", "backward" and "reactionary" influences. Most Third World socialist countries have therefore moved rapidly to implement policies to improve the position of women especially in areas where these "feudal" influences are thought to be most detrimental to the wider goals of the socialist state.

In Democratic Yemen these wider goals and the strategies adopted in order to realise them were embodied in the NLF's post-1967 planning. The first three-year plan stressed the urgency of stimulating rapid economic development with the state assuming a leading role in economic life. The nationalisation of the "commanding

4

heights" of the economy was to be accompanied by a policy giving industrialisation maximum support. At the same time, the agrarian sector was to be transformed through the expropriation of the larger private holdings, the rationalisation of production, and where possible, through the establishment of state farms and co-operatives. In broad outline the policies amounted to the establishment of a planned economy with a strong state sector and considerable government intervention at the level of prices, wages and production, a model found in most countries in the socialist bloc.

The NLF was also committed to profound social change as a means of accelerating and complementing the transformation in the economic sphere. These changes included not only the fulfilment of the welfare aims of the state — the provision of housing, health and educational facilities — but also the mobilisation of an adequate supply of labour to meet the growing requirements generated by government policies. Within this context the mobilisation of women into the labour force had an instrumental aspect to it as well as being a matter of principle.

This is not to imply that the principle itself was unimportant. Socialist states and parties have everywhere given support to the principle of sexual equality, and this is reflected in socialist doctrine, policies and legislation. In Democratic Yemen Lenin's *On the emancipation of women* and Engel's *Origin of the family, private property and the State* exist in translation, and extracts from these texts or echoes of their main themes sometimes appear in policy documents as explanations or validations of the strategies pursued. This is indicative of something of more general significance, since these writings are seen as providing the basis of official theorising on women and contain the core assumptions which underlie the conventional policies adopted by socialist states in relation to women. The most influential theses derive from Engel's theory of women's subordination contained in *The Origin* and can be summed up in the following propositions: women cannot be emancipated unless they (a) participate in social production and are (b) freed from the "domestic slavery" of the home. In order to accomplish (a) some responsibility for women's conventional duties in the home must be shouldered by the state; in order to help accomplish both (a) and (b) the family must cease to function as an economic or productive unit of society.

The policy implications of these propositions were set out most clearly in the resolutions of the second Congress of the Communist International in 1920 which in many respects, was the constitutive meeting of the Communist movement. This emphasised the following measures: bringing women out of the home and into the economy; reorganising peasant households that keep women in subservient positions; providing equal opportunities for women; and ensuring appropriate working conditions to "satisfy the particular needs of the female organism and the moral and spiritual needs of women as mothers" (Jancar, 1978).

These policies have formed the basis of socialist countries' programmes relating to women throughout the world. Despite certain limitations and the considerable problems of implementation faced by poorer countries, there can be little doubt that if carried out, they represent a major step forward. But the question arises as to how successful a poor country such as Democratic Yemen has been in implementing these policies and in improving the position of women generally. The subsequent sections will attempt to approach an answer to this question by analysing in detail the different aspects of state policies on women as they have been implemented in Democratic Yemen. An attempt will be made to assess the strengths and weaknesses of the record

5

so far, bearing in mind the conditions of extreme scarcity that inevitably restrict the realm of freedom within which these policies are enacted.

3. Islam

We will begin with what must be one of the most difficult and controversial areas of social reform, that which is directed at religion. Despite recent moves in some countries to reverse the process, there has occurred in most Muslim countries a gradual loosening of the ties between organised religion and the state. This has been a slow and uneven process both across and within countries, yet despite the differences between them in points of detail, most Muslim countries have undergone a process of gradual secularisation, wherein the institutions of the state, education and the law have acquired some degree of independence from the religious authorities, involving varying degrees of reform. As far as the position of women is concerned, the impact of religious orthodoxy on the law, in particular on the Family Laws and laws of personal status, is a factor of the utmost significance, and here too, state policies in the Muslim world are extremely diverse. While most Muslim countries have secularised that part of their legal system pertaining to commerce, finance, criminal and penal law, many have left the Family Law and the codes on personal status relatively untouched; and it is precisely within these religious codes that the position of women is defined as legally subordinate to that of men. The religious influence and derivation of the codes thus allows the subordination of women to be legitimised in terms of doctrinal orthodoxy as well as making it difficult to bring about reforms in this area (see Beck and Keddie, 1979). This raises the more general question of the part played by Islam, as a system of beliefs, in the perpetuation of sexual inequality.

It would be facile, of course, to attribute women's subordination in the Arab world solely to the influence of Islam. Women in other regions of the Third World suffer from many of the forms of discrimination which Muslim women are subjected to, and such customs as polygamy, the brideprice and child marriage are by no means confined to the Muslim world but are linked more generally to certain pre-capitalist property firms and economic systems which have existed in both East and West. In Muslim countries, it is often the case moreover that the ideology of women's inferiority and the customs within which it is articulated are a fusion of religious and customary or tribal laws, some of the latter denying the rights given to women by the Koran and other sources, especially the *Hadith* or sayings of the Prophet. Similarly, as Islamic reformers have been concerned to point out, the explicit religious content within this ideological ensemble is generally made up of selective and interpretative readings of the Koran and the *Hadith*. Such interpretations have tended to disregard some of the more humanitarian provisions of the sacred texts particularly in the matter of women's rights. Other readings have interpreted ambiguous statements as clear mandates and have legislated as if they were such. For example, although the Koran sanctions polygamy and divorce by repudiation, it none the less attaches certain conditions designed to bestow some rights on divorced women. Minimal though these are, they are often ignored in practice. And although the strict seclusion of women is not compulsory for believers any more than are cliteridectomy, veiling and other customs found in many Islamic societies, Koranic verses merely favouring these practices have often been interpreted as mandatory (see El Saadawi, 1979; Mernissi, 1975). It is therefore a matter of some dispute as to how far the sexual inequalities enshrined within the traditional legal codes derive from Islamic doctrine itself and how far they derive from an incorrect interpretation of the doctrine.

Despite these qualifications there can be little doubt that the ideological ensemble which articulates women's inferiority in many Muslim societies claims a religious derivation and on the basis of this derivation establishes its legitimacy. Although the Koran was in advance of most of the other world religions in according women any rights at all, these rights were not equal to men's. In certain formulations, the Koran and the *Hadith* represent women as inferior to men and this inferiority is institutionalised in the orthodox legal codes and practices. These give women only half as much as men in property rights[10] and define women as juridical minors, in a subordinate position to men and requiring male guardians. At the same time, men are accorded a place of privilege and authority: the Koran states categorically that "Men stand superior to women in that God hath preferred the one over the other".[11] Elsewhere women are characterised as less responsible and more susceptible to distraction. This often forms the rationale behind the exclusion of women from positions of social responsibility whether in the economic, social or political sphere. Similarly, whereas a man's judgement on the matter of divorce is unquestioned and he need only pronounce the words "I divorce thee" three times to secure a divorce, a woman must press her case in the courts and must produce witnesses to substantiate it. Thus, juridical inequality, and the ideology of women's inferiority *together with* the practice of seclusion ensure that women are generally excluded from positions of responsibility in civil society and from most aspects of economic life, except where such participation is mediated through and subordinate to men, as for example, when women work on familial land.[12]

Given the marked gender inequality in many Muslim societies and the role of Islamic orthodoxy in sustaining it, no government that was genuinely committed to the emancipation of women could leave the *shariat* and *urf* legal codes intact. Thus, although Islam is the state religion of Democratic Yemen, the present government has sought, like such other Arab states as the Syrian Arab Republic, Iraq, Turkey and Tunisia, to reform some of the main inequalities enshrined in the traditional codes. At the same time it has progressively eroded the juridical power of religious leaders and has partially transferred this power to agencies of the state.[13] This latter process began during the liberation struggle when the revolutionaries moved against the *Sadaa* and other religious leaders in the areas around Radfan where they were based, expropriating their lands without compensation and forcing the more conservative elements into exile. After the revolution, *waqf* (religious) lands were placed under state administration and those religious leaders who did not leave the country were given the option of either surrendering their posts or continuing to occupy them as employees of the state. At the same time a secular legal system gradually came into force in the hinterland. Previously, secular laws had existed in Aden because of its status as a colony but *shariat* personal laws were still in force for the Muslim community. The reform of religious practices has therefore been one of the many planks of the government's attempt to transform the society, and at the same time to improve the position of women. It was also an integral part of a wider process of legal reform which we will now examine in more detail.

7

4. Women and the law: Personal status, marriage and the family

1. The constitutional reforms

Although one of the earliest initiatives of the government of the first President, Qahtan al-Shaabi, was to found a women's organisation in 1968 called the General Union of Yemeni Women (GUYW), little else was done in the immediate post-Independence period to promote changes in the position of women. Within the government it was the left-wing radicals who were chiefly concerned with the question of women's rights, and it was not until this faction came to unchallenged power in June 1969, over a year and a half after Independence, that more concerted efforts were made to encourage women to participate in, and benefit from, the revolutionary process (General Union of Yemeni Women, 1976). The 1970 Constitution laid out in broad outline the government's attitude towards women and provided the framework within which legal reforms would be inscribed. The Constitutional reforms addressed women in terms of two main roles envisaged for them by the revolutionary government — as "producers" and as "mothers". Article 7 which describes the political basis of the revolution as an "alliance between the working class, the peasants, intelligentsia and petty-bourgeoisie" goes on to add that "Soldiers, *women* and students are regarded as part of this alliance by *virtue of their membership in the productive forces of the people* " (emphasis added). Women are therefore recognised as part of the "working people" and the Constitution, in giving all citizens the right to work and in regarding work as "an obligation in the case of all able-bodied citizens", calls on women not yet involved in "productive work" to enter this sphere and by implication to challenge the restrictions of seclusion. At the same time, the Constitution promised to "strengthen the family status and (to) protect mother and child" (Article 29). Lest this exhortation to preserve the family and encourage women to work be thought contradictory, certain provisions were to be made specifically for the working mother: Article 36 promises that "The State shall also ensure special protection for working women and children by granting paid leave for expectant mothers ... (and) ... The State shall establish nurseries and kindergartens and other means of care and custody (of children) ..."

These statutes and provisions marked in themselves a considerable advance on previous government policy in a number of respects, but it was the articles declaring juridical and political equality for all citizens that ushered in even more profound changes in the position of women. Article 34 which states that "All citizens are equal in their rights and obligations ... (and) all are equal in the eye of the law" represented a break with previous laws and customs under which women had had inferior rights to men. Constitutional reform in this case implied at the very least a radical change in legal status if only, as yet, a formal one. Article 36 went some way towards making it more than merely a formal commitment by affirming that "The State shall guarantee equal rights for men and women in all fields of political, economic and social scope (sic) and shall provide in a progressive manner the conditions necessary for realising that equality". Among the conditions provided for in the Constitution were the expansion of the women's union to assist women in gaining their rights, the extension of education and literacy programmes to women, the encouragement of women's political participation and their mass entry into social production. In subsequent sections we shall examine these different aspects of government attempts to

8

transform the position of women. Here we will focus on the attempts to provide the legal pre-conditions for achieving these aims.

2. Legal reform

The progressive extension of new penal and civil codes to the hinterland brought some improvement in the position of women. Whereas in the past, crimes against women were regarded as family or tribal affairs and harsh punishment could be meted out to disobedient daughters or wives by men who were never themselves brought to trial, women began to gain for the first time the chance of attaining a hearing in the People's Courts and could count on some support from their local Popular Defence Committees and the Women's Union.

But even more important in improving women's position was the 1974 Family Law, which aimed directly at transforming traditional inequalities in the Muslim family itself. The Family Law, like the Constitution, was discussed in the press and in open meetings around the country before being promulgated. The draft law was drawn up in 1971 and over a period of three years amendments were incorporated into it on the basis of the popular response and the reaction of the mass organisations.[14] In this it followed a similar course to the Cuban Family Law which was passed in 1975 after having been widely debated in public meetings.

The Law was modelled on the Tunisian family codes of 1956 but went some way further than these. In Muslim countries, reforming legislation of this kind tends to be justified in terms of a specific interpretation of the religious texts. In Democratic Yemen, the co-operation of prominent *Qadis* (religious jurists) was obtained for the formulation of the Law, although some observers claim that a Marxist bias is evident in attempts to remove class privilege from the codes (see Ghanem, 1976). The preamble to the Law began by denouncing "the vicious state of affairs which prevails in the family" and justified reform on the grounds that it "opens vast fields of creative work and equal revolutionary relations which lead to the increase of production, development and innovation". The section on marriage and betrothal announced the end of some of the traditional inequalities in marriage: "Marriage is a contract between a man and a women who are equal in rights and duties, and is based on mutual understanding and respect with the object of building up the cohesive family which is regarded as the foundation stone of the society."

The specific reforms introduced by the Law included the following:

(1) Marriages were to come under greater state control. Article 6 states that the marriage contract is only effective when registered with the public notary and signed in the presence of two witnesses. This helps to ensure that some of the provisions of the Family Law (age, consent) are observed.

(2) Arranged marriages were to be made illegal. As Article 3 states: "The family of any girl whose engagement is sought by an individual may not consent to the engagement without first having consulted the girl, and with her agreement". Although this requirement is stipulated in one of the *Hadiths* of the Prophet, it was almost never observed in practice.

(3) Whereas there had previously been widespread child marriage in the countryside, the minimum legal age was fixed at 16 years for women and at 18 for men (Article 7). In a further move to prevent the marriage of young women to much older

9

men the age difference was limited to 20 years for a woman under 35 (Article 9).

(4)   Whereas men had previously been allowed to marry up to four wives, the Law now stipulated that men could, like women, have only one spouse, except in certain exceptional circumstances (barrenness, incurable disease) (Article 11).

(5)   In order further to reduce family control over marriages, the amount of the brideprice or *mahr* was limited to 100 Yemeni Dinars (about twice an average white-collar monthly salary) (Article 18). In this way it was hoped to remove a conventional form of class control over marriages, while at the same time making it easier for women to escape from a bad marriage by repaying the brideprice herself. As the preamble to the Law stated, women in the previous situation had been "in the hands of the highest bidder".

(6)   Whereas men were previously expected to be the main breadwinners, Article 17 of the new codes stipulated that both spouses "shall participate in bearing the expenses of marriage and establishing the conjugal home according to their means". And both must henceforth "share in bearing the costs of their married life" unless one of the parties is unable to, whereupon the other has to assume responsibility.

(7)   One of the constitutive inequalities in most Muslim societies is the differential right to divorce. Men have had the traditional right to repudiation (*talaq*) and have been able to divorce women at will. Divorce has been much more difficult for women to obtain and has involved recourse to the local courts, appearance in which is regarded as shameful for women. Under the new Law unilateral divorce of this kind is prohibited and all divorces have to be processed through the courts (Article 25). The grounds for divorce are, with some minor differences, now applicable to both men and women.

(8)   Mothers acquired the right of custody over their children for a more extended period than is usual (until the age of 10 for a boy and 15 for a girl). The fear of losing their children at an early age was said by Women's Union officials to be one of the worst aspects of divorce as far as women were concerned.

The Family Law therefore established the basis for a quite different family structure and radically altered relations within it. The traditional control exercised by the head of the family over marriages and hence over familial property was in effect outlawed, and the control over daughters was thereby eroded. In addition, the equalisation of conjugal rights and the ending of unilateral divorce and polygamy strengthened women's position within this new family form.

The new family of Democratic Yemen was to be monogamous, and it was hoped that it would be less unstable than its predecessor, since this instability was held to arise in large part from the profound inequalities existing within it. However, it would be erroneous to see the new Law as establishing complete legal equality between men and women, since some relics of traditional Islamic practice have remained. A man can take a second spouse under exceptional and certified circumstances such as barrenness, whilst a woman cannot do the same on grounds of impotence. Similarly a woman can be divorced for barrenness but nothing is said in the Law as to whether a man can be divorced for impotence. A woman who was divorced is still prohibited for the stipulated period (Iddat) of up to 90 days from remarrying, whereas a man is exempted from such proscriptions. This Islamic injunction is designed to protect men from the possible loss of an heir who might have been conceived before the divorce and who, if the woman remarried, would be considered the child of her new spouse. Although arranged marriages are outlawed the brideprice remains, albeit with a lower upper limit. Finally, as far as property transmission is concerned, *shariat* law continues to prevail and the discrimination against women that it embodies therefore persists. Faced with these disparities, legal advisers of Democratic Yemen claim that the Family Law is continually under review; they report that the Women's Union has been pressing for the removal of surviving anomalies and for further improvements in the legal position of women.

An important aspect of the Family Law is that it is located within a precisely formulated policy; here the major aim is not just the full equality of men and women, but the strengthening of the family unit which is considered as the "basic cell" of society. The result of (almost) equalising divorce procedures has been to make it as difficult for a man as for a woman to obtain a divorce and it is clear from the Law, and from the practice of the courts, that divorces are only granted in the very last resort. Government policy is aimed at reinforcing the family and this is seen as a necessary component of the over-all strategy of social development. This is clearly stated in the Constitution and reiterated in the Family Law. However, according to a woman judge who specialised in the administration of justice in family matters, the courts have received large numbers of requests for divorce since the Family Law gave women the right to divorce in 1974. According to colonial government reports divorce rates have always been high in Democratic Yemen, but in the past these were mainly initiated by men; now women form a large proportion of those suing for divorce. The official view is that women's dissatisfaction with their marriage partners can be explained as a result of unsatisfactory early marriages, their increased financial independence, and desertion by emigrant husbands who have remarried abroad and abandoned their families back home. Although initially sympathetic to the petitions for divorce, the government became concerned that the rate of divorce was too high and the social implications of instability too great for it to be allowed to continue unchecked. Although no figures have been released, officials believed the divorce rate to have increased substantially since the pre-Independence period and it is this increase that is said to lie behind the government's decision to take measures making divorce more difficult to obtain.

Potential divorces now have to wait between several months and a year before their case is heard at court, in order to reconsider whether they should continue to press their suit. In the meantime the Women's Union or the Popular Defence Committees act as marriage guidance counsellors and try to persuade the couple against divorce. Before a case even goes to court, these bodies have to be persuaded that the litigant has a reasonable case; otherwise, it does not go forward. A further disincentive, particularly for women, is that alimony is granted only for one year, after which the chances of support from the state, although theoretically possible, are minimal. After a year husbands are under no further obligation and a divorced woman generally has to rely, as in the past, on the beneficence of her kinfolk. Foreseeing this, her relatives may try to dissuade her from divorcing in the first place or urge her to remarry. The kin network thus joins the government bodies in discouraging the break-up of the family.[15]

Another aspect of state policy relating to the family is that of population control. As would be expected, there was not in the past any state intervention in favour of family planning. Contraception is not as strongly disapproved of by Islam as it is by Catholicism, but given the sparse medical facilities, contraceptive devices other than from popular sources were available on the market in only small supplies until the

11

1970s. In the ports of Aden and Mukalla women have had some access to contraception as these were items which were imported, initially for the use of visiting foreigners, but which gradually became more widely available. In recent years however, a new pattern has emerged. A study of 1,000 women attending a mother and child health clinic in 1975 shows that 42 per cent of the women used some form of contraception before attending the clinic; 90 per cent of these women were on the pill and most of them had started taking it within the last three years (see Democratic Yemen, MCH Services, 1977). Other forms of contraception are available in small supplies on the market but at a price the majority of the people of Democratic Yemen would be reluctant to pay, and it is doubtful how far supplies penetrate beyond the main urban areas. Sterilisation for women is discouraged, and is carried out on men only in rare cases. A major factor influencing state policy in this area is the labour situation. Democratic Yemen claims to have a marked shortage of labour and the main emphasis of the birth control policy is not to reduce the over-all rate of population growth which currently runs at over 3 per cent per annum; on the contrary the second five-year Health Plan is resolutely committed to population growth. The primary aim is rather to space births and so decrease the maternal and infant mortality rates, which are high at 10 per 10,000 births and 152 per 1,000 live births respectively. It is in the light of this requirement that after 1974 contraceptives began to be selectively distributed through government health centres.

On the related matter of abortion, state policy is still not precisely formulated. In 1977 the Minister of Health reported that it was still "under discussion" between his Ministry, the Ministry of Justice and the Women's Union. Until now it has been neither legal nor illegal. As with contraception, Islam has not adopted a position hostile to abortion comparable to that found in Christianity, but some Muslim authorities do forbid it (it was, for example, banned in post-revolutionary Iran).

Although there is little evidence available, officials asserted that the incidence of abortion was low in Democratic Yemen, the annual total of those carried out with official permission being between 100 and 150. Other sources, however, suggested a somewhat higher rate although these would not necessarily have come to the attention of the authorities.[16] The grounds acceptable at the present time are limited to medical reasons, to cases where women have too many children, and to some cases where extreme social complications might result. As the Minister of Health made clear, this is "a problem of the future" , but it is unlikely that Democratic Yemen, with its objective shortage of labour and medical facilities, will allow anything but a restricted abortion policy.

Two main problems confront the government in the field of juridical reform. First, the question of popularising the Law, and secondly that of how to enforce the new legislation; merely to promulgate laws is no guarantee that they will be effective. As far as the first question is concerned, we have seen that in drafting and circulating the new laws for discussion, a major effort was made, as in Cuba during the same phase, to diffuse knowledge of the law at the formulation stage through public meetings and to encourage some measure of popular participation. Even now, after the promulgation of the laws, work still goes on to inform people about their rights and obligations through public meetings, newspaper coverage, television (in Aden), and radio broadcasts. The content of discussions at local level, which are led by Party members, Women's Union officials and the other mass organisations, is fed back to the government committees who make recommendations for changes to the Supreme

12

People's Council. In this way the government hopes to popularise the new laws and to further their voluntary acceptance through persuading people of their role in formulating law and of the superiority of the new over the previous system.

A major obstacle in the way of this process is the fear of opposition to the reforms on religious grounds whether by more conservative Arab states or by internal forces. Criticisms coming from these quarters are directed in particular at the efforts to transform the position of women. The government's appointment of women as judges has frequently been denounced as a contravention of religious principles, even though there is nothing in the Koran which explicitly forbids this. Some conservative Arab states have in the past condemned Democratic Yemen for encouraging the erosion of *purdah* restrictions and have called on them in Pan Arab congresses to segregate educational establishments. While the danger of a traditional and religious backlash over this issue is ever present, government officials insist that it should not be exaggerated, both because the reforms are genuinely popular and because conservative religious feeling in Democratic Yemen has never been as strong as in some other Arab states. Be that as it may, Democratic Yemen is vulnerable to pressure from both inside and outside the country and for this reason it has been at pains to demonstrate its continued adherence to Islam. While seeking to reform social practices it has retained Islam as the state religion, observing religious ceremonies and holidays and teaching the doctrine in schools, albeit in such a way as to yield a more enlightened interpretation.

Enforcement of the law is recognised by officials as being extremely problematic. Evasion is common, especially in the rural areas where traditional and familial authority remain strong and where customary modes of procedure continue to be favoured. Although all marriages are supposed to be registered by the State, and individuals are under no official obligations to complement this with a religious marriage, many people of Democratic Yemen still opt overwhelmingly for it by preference.[17] Similarly, Women's Union officials in the rural areas claimed that arranged marriages below the age of consent were still common owing in part to the difficulty of providing the age of the bride-to-be. Birth registries in many areas do not date back far enough to allow suspicious officials to prove that a marriage is illegal. Although the consent of both principals is required before a marriage contract is concluded by the state, reluctant marriage partners rarely defy their families' wishes. Although it was claimed that there was an increasing number of cases where the principals did resist, the control kin exercise over marriage and the family has not on the whole been surrendered.

However, the government has not refrained from using severe measures against those who violate the law, as is illustrated by an episode which took place in the 4th Governorate in 1978. A young girl from a prominent Seyyid family in Haban, had refused to marry the man her grandfather had chosen for her. Instead she eloped with a man of an inferior caste. Her grandfather together with her mother and brother tracked her down and had her murdered and secretly buried. But some local people, who suspected that a crime had been committed, reported their suspicions to the authorities who mounted a search for the young girl's body, and found it. The villagers, on hearing the full details of the crime, seized the old man and dragged him through the streets in a procession; he was eventually brought to trial and sentenced to death by the People's courts. The whole episode was well publicised in the press and on radio and at public meetings so that appropriate lessons could be drawn. The attitude

13

of the authorities and of the villagers was significant in that it marked a radical change in mores; a few years earlier such a murder would have gone unpunished and would indeed have been regarded as the natural prerogative of an elder whose will had been disobeyed by a woman.[18]

One can pose the question of how successful the legal reforms have been, given the over-all position of women in Democratic Yemen prior to the changes. There can be no doubt that the legal and constitutional reforms in Democratic Yemen have been important instruments in helping to improve the position of women, although it will be a long time before women's inferior social position radically changes. Women of Democratic Yemen who expressed an opinion to me on the matter of their reformed legal status were unanimously enthusiastic about the changes; although many of them acknowledged the existence of paternal and familial tutelage, they felt that they had been provided with a basis on which to build.

It is worth remarking that the new laws have refrained from attacking such institutions as veiling or, for that matter, practices such as cliteridectomy (*khitan*) which remain legal in Democratic Yemen. As far as the latter is concerned official opinion is that it is not a problem since it is not widely practiced in Democratic Yemen. Where it does exist it is thought that it will soon die out with the extension of medical facilities to the rural areas and the erosion of the power of traditional doctors (*hakim*).

Veiling and the seclusion of women are similarly tolerated on the grounds that they are an anachronism, which if left to objective forces will soon disappear.[19] In 1972, as part of the general popular mobilisations in support of government policies women are reported to have marched through the streets proclaiming the end of veiling, and while the government gave some support to this campaign it now prefers to discourage veiling in a more indirect manner. Certainly, stringent measures against the veil such as those adopted in Soviet Central Asia in 1927, in Turkey under Ataturk or in Iran under Reza Shah, have never been adopted. The policy has been to avoid provoking a violent reaction by refraining from directly confronting the issue. Indirectly, tacit support is given to ending the practice by encouraging the wearing of school and workplace uniforms; many government officials and Women's Union cadres in Aden go about their tasks unveiled, wearing skirts, headscarfs, long-sleeved blouses, but they often wear the *sheidor* at women's meetings in order to avoid alienating some of the more conservative members of the audience. However, without discussing the symbolic meaning of the veil and without confronting the question of the control men exercise over women through the practice of seclusion, there is a danger that these fundamental structures within which women's subordination is inscribed will not simply wither away under the dual pressure of objective forces and a hoped-for subjective transformation of popular attitudes.

NOTES

1) See Halliday (1974) for an account of the Independence movement and for the history and social structure of Democratic Yemen.
2) The towns and their immediate surroundings fell under the jurisdiction of the sultans and emirs and beneath them were ranked the other main social groups. In the Hadramaut area a more clearly defined caste structure developed with the *Sadah* at the top and the poor population of labourers and artisans, the *Akhdam* at the bottom. The *Sadah* or *Hashimites* claimed descent from the Prophet Mohammed, a status which gave them access to considerable resources as well as local power and prestige. Between these two groups were ranked in strict order a variety of other strata, differentiated by the clothes they wore, the nature and place of residence, burial grounds and address forms as well as other forms of ritualised behaviour. Bujra's (1971) analysis of a Hadrami town is the most detailed sociological study of Democratic Yemen's pre-revolutionary social order.
3) This is similar to the Iranian *chador* from which it is said to derive. It is a loose black silk or rayon head-to-toe covering.
4) In Democratic Yemen, as in other parts of the Middle East, the wearing of the veil or *sheidor* is often regarded as a symbol of status. Previously restricted to high-born urban women it has now spread fairly evenly across the urban class structure even though it has by no means become a universal practice. Bedouin women and peasant women do not as a rule veil themselves although they may on occasion don the *sheidor* when they travel to the towns. When asked if she ever used the *sheidor* or the veil an old peasant woman said with some pride: "The veil is for the town woman who sits all day in her house. It is not for we women who work."
5) This description of the sexual division of labour is corroborated by such diverse sources as the documents of the General Union of Yemeni Women, Stark (1936) and interviews by the author with rural women.
6) *Qat* or "Cathula edulis" is grown in both the Yemen Arab Republic and Democratic Yemen and in the north is taken by most men and some mainly rural women as part of their daily relaxation and social life. In the south, consumption has been restricted to Fridays and Thursday afternoons, but it remains a popular, if expensive luxury. At one sitting four Yemeni Dinars worth of *qat* can be chewed, i.e. about a fifth of the monthly wage of a factory worker. Since it is mostly men who engage in this practice this amounts to a rather obvious male privilege.
7) According to Women's Union officials in Dhaleh near the border with the Yemen Arab Republic, the birth of two daughters in a row was regarded as sufficient grounds for divorce in the area.
8) In the more deeply conservative areas of the Hadramaut region, Doreen Ingrams (1970) observed that at puberty girls were not even allowed to be seen by women who were not of the immediate family.
9) These practices were singled out for special condemnation by the then President, Salem Robaya Ali at the first Congress of the Women's Union in 1974. (See *The Documents of the General Union of Yemeni Women* (Aden, 1976).)

10) "For the male the like of the portion of two females." *Koran*: Surah, 4, verses 9–12.
11) *Koran*: Surah, 4, verse 58.
12) Fatima Mernissi (1975) has drawn attention to the control over female sexuality which is implied by Islamic doctrine and by the more conservative interpretations of it. She argues that fear of the power of female sexuality justifies the imposition of strict segregation between the sexes and more than any other ideology ensures as far as women's class position permits, their physical confinement to the domestic sphere and their almost complete exclusion from public life.
13) A similar process occurred in Soviet Central Asia after the revolution. See Massell (1974) for a full account, based on official Russian sources.
14) Several witnesses, including one of the notaries involved in the drafting of the codes, have attested to the fact that women in these public discussions tended to be more in favour of radical reform measures than men.
15) This is gradually changing as divorced women are encouraged to enter wage labour.
16) The same MCH report shows that 27.7 per cent of the women registered had had at least one abortion; 13.8 per cent had had one abortion; 8 per cent two; 3 per cent three; and 2.9 per cent between four and eight. The report, however, does not say how these were obtained.
17) This was confirmed by officials and non-officials alike, although some interviewees claimed that the incidence of religious marriages was gradually declining in Aden.
18) In January 1981 the Deputy Prime Minister, Ali Al-Beid, was relieved of his post. One of the grounds was his violation of the Family Law by taking a second wife.
19) See the statements on this contained in Molyneux (1980).

CHAPTER I

POLITICAL INVOLVEMENT

Until the 1950s, women, along with the rest of the population, were largely excluded from any involvement in political life. It was only then that the growth of Arab nationalism began to exacerbate some of the tensions already present in Democratic Yemen society, drawing men and women into political activity often for the first time. In Aden, women joined demonstrations in support of Nasser's position in the Suez crisis of 1956; women school teachers went on strike in 1957 to protest against what they saw as biased pro-British curricula, and women began to be drawn into political organisations when they sprang up in the fifties and sixties. The women who joined these organisations were often from the better educated and better-off sectors of Adeni society, who might have disapproved of their daughters' involvement, but who were lenient enough to tolerate it provided that it remained within certain limits.[1]

Despite the increased involvement of women in political activities, the issue of greater equality for women was raised in only a few organisations. Even these operated with a limited conception of what this would entail and such issues were overshadowed by the struggle for national liberation which was seen as the overriding priority. Some women's organisations did exist during the Independence struggle but these were political arms of nationalist tendencies rather than women's organisations as such. The first ever women's organisation in Aden was the Aden Women's Club founded in 1954 by Mrs. Hinkenbotham, the wife of the British High Commissioner. Little is known about this organisation except that it campaigned against the veil and was involved in certain forms of social work. In 1958 it became the Aden Women's Society under the leadership of a wealthy woman of what was formerly known as South Yemen and was able to recruit an all-Arab membership. As the Society soon became identified with the more right-wing nationalist currents struggling for Adeni secession, the question of women's rights receded. During the early sixties a new organisation emerged calling itself the Arab Women's Society. Whereas the previous group had been drawn from the more wealthy members of Adeni society, the new membership was predominantly middle class and petty-bourgeois. It too was founded as a branch of the Arab Nationalist (Nasserist) movement in Aden and when this split into Nasserist and revolutionary factions in 1962–63 the women's organisation did so too.

In the four years of the guerrilla struggle against the United Kingdom many women played an active auxiliary role. As in Algeria's Independence movement, the 200 or so women who worked with or in the NLF acted as messengers, led demonstrations and smuggled arms. In the mountains women played a back-up role in the rural guerrilla warfare carrying military supplies and food to the front. There were, however, no large populated areas under permanent guerrilla control within which practical reforms could be effected. A few women in the mountains participated in armed actions and there are one or two official heroines of the revolution such as Daara, from the Radfan area where the revolution began, and Hadiga al Haushabi who

17

became a unit commander. But there was no systematic involvement of women in the guerrilla forces and few women "martyrs" are counted among the victims of the revolutionary struggle. However, women in Democratic Yemen were to be rewarded for their participation with a post-Independence policy package designed to eliminate the worst inequalities in the law and society in general.

Since Independence the government has tried to promote a high level of political participation among women through electoral mechanisms, drawing women into the various political organisations and state administration, and by setting up a Women's Union. Women were given the chance to vote for the first time in the country's history in the 1977 local council elections, and they achieved a fairly high turn-out with women comprising over one-third of the voters in Aden. In the First Governorate (the area in and around Aden) a special effort had been made to field women candidates. Ten women in all stood for election, all of them members of the Women's Union. Eight of them were elected, a result of which the Union was particularly proud.

The political education of women is carried out in three ways: through general mass meetings organised by the Party at the place of work, through the mass organisations, and at special Party schools where selected cadres from the Party or from the mass organisations are sent for periods of up to a year. After they qualify, they are sent out as cadres, often to the rural areas, to carry on organisational work. In general it is true to say that women officials of whatever organisation are concerned principally with organising and mobilising other women, inevitably perhaps in a society where the legacy of seclusion is still strong.

However, women's participation in political activity is still low in comparison with men's. In conformity with the pattern found in most societies, the largest concentration of women is at the base of the political structure. In Democratic Yemen women are present in the Party and in most of the mass organisations — the trade unions, youth and student organisations, the Popular Defence Councils, and of course, the Women's Union. Membership figures are incomplete but officials claimed that about one-third of the General Union of Yemeni Workers' membership of 84,000 was comprised of women. Since membership in this organisation is automatic for workers, it does not give us any indication of how many women are active in the Union. My own research (see Part II) indicates that a very small percentage of women workers (0.1 per cent) have any role at all as officials in the Workers' Union. This impression is confirmed by the fact that of the Union's 96 full-time officials none is a woman, and this is disappointing in view of the existence of factories both in Aden and in the hinterland which have a majority of women workers. From the little information available, it would appear that women are more active in the Popular Defence Councils and the student and youth organisations, although there are no over-all membership figures to confirm this.

Where women have acceded to a middle-ranking leadership role in those organisations, they are often charged with a rather restricted range of concerns and ones which tend to confirm the "traditional" roles women are associated with. Women cadres in the Popular Defence Committees were, for example, responsible mainly in the areas of social welfare. Officials claimed that of the total membership of the Party, 10 per cent were women. Few of these are in the highest echelons of the Party. The Presidential Council and the 16 member Politburo are all male; and of the approximately 68 member Central Committee only five are women. A few more "candidates" or probationary members increase the percentage slightly, but it still

18

remains low. This is also the case with the Supreme People's Council whose 101 members include only a handful of women. This body has reserved seats for members who have been elected by various constituencies; 15 members are elected by the trade union movement, 86 are chosen by the local councils in general elections, and the Women's Union also has some representatives but it is not known how many. Finally, as with the Politburo, the Council of Ministers, a powerful policy-making body which comprises 15 people, does not include any women, because no woman has as yet held the post of minister.

The organisation with primary responsibility for mobilising women into political activity is the General Union of Yemeni Women. The Women's Union is a mass organisation of the Party and is organised in the same way as are the trade unions, the peasants union and the youth and student organisations. These bodies are controlled by the Yemeni Socialist Party (YSP) through the Secretary for Mass Organisations, who sits on the Central Committee and directs mass organisation policy. Hence, while the membership of the Women's Union elect their governing committee and discuss policy, this is within the limits laid down by the Central Committee. Members of the Women's Union are represented in the leading bodies of Party and State. There is at least one member of the GUYW at every level of the Party structure. Similarly, the Union has the right to nominate a quota of members to the legislative bodies — the local councils in each governorate, and the Supreme People's Council, the highest legislative body. Women also stand in their own right for election to these bodies. But in practice the candidates for election and the policies discussed in these councils are under the control of the YSP. In this way a high degree of integration of Party and State is maintained.

The Women's Union (GUYW) was founded in 1968 and during the early seventies operated from three main centres, in Aden, Lehej and in the Hadramaut. Its initial concerns were the literacy campaign and the Family Law. Women's Union members and supporters were involved in teaching women how to read and write and in persuading them or their families of the importance of women's education. At the same time, the Family Law was being circulated for discussion across the nation and the Women's Union presided over meetings, monitoring reactions to the proposed changes and playing an active role in the redrafting of the Law which was finally promulgated in 1974.

The activities of the GUYW as a national organisation date from the conference held at Seyun in 1974. Under the banner "Yemeni women shall struggle against ignorance and for the love of work", a proper organisational structure and official representation was formed in all six governorates. At this conference the Union was given a 35 member general secretariat which was to form the Union leadership. Each of these members heads a committee with specific responsibilities — internal relations, external affairs, information and culture, social affairs, finance and administration and economic affairs. This structure is replicated at the local level throughout the country.

As with the Popular Defence Councils, members are recruited into the GUYW at their place of residence. The Union claims a membership of 14,926 — 915 of whom are workers in manufacturing, 528 are rural workers, mainly members of co-operatives and state farms, 253 are government employees, some are students and the rest, i.e. 89 per cent are "housewives". This preponderance of home-based members may in part reflect the special efforts made by the government's literacy campaign to reach women who were still in seclusion. It is reasonable to suppose that many such women joined the Union during or after their literacy courses. The small percentage of employed women reflects a wider social and economic reality as we shall see later. The majority of the membership are under 30 years old and the Women's Union has found it difficult to attract older women. It is striking that despite their relatively young age, so many remain "housewives". Members pay a subscription fee of 100 *fils* a month (about 15 pence) if they are engaged in paid work, and 50 *fils* if they do not. At present the Union receives a subsidy from the government, but it eventually hopes to be fully self-supporting.

The Women's Union sees its main function as helping the state to integrate women into economic activity. To this end it has been an active supporter of the literacy campaigns and a promoter of women's employment opportunities. The Union has special responsibility for providing training facilities for women and has set up a variety of schemes designed to generate both rural and urban employment. One such scheme, set up as part of the activities for International Women's Year in 1976, involved the establishment of six "Technical Training Centres" for women in different parts of the country. These centres provided training in a variety of skills, including the more conventional ones such as typing and sewing, but mechanical and technical skills were also taught. By 1977 the centres had trained over 1,500 women, and the project has been relatively successful despite the problems that it has encountered. These problems were reported to include a high drop-out rate among the students, and the difficulty of persuading parents to allow their daughters to move to the centres, as the training period involves living on the premises for between three months and a year. In some regions, opposition to the project by families and traditionalist elements was said to be considerable and as a result two of the six centres had to be closed down.

In addition to the centres, the Women's Union sponsors the establishment of workshops and small factories which provide training and employment for women. It has set up a number of sewing co-operatives, and some 70 per cent of the women who work there have been trained by the Union. The co-operatives make women's and children's clothes which are sold in the Union shop in Aden or distributed through Union networks in the rural areas. The Union also has a part share in at least two factories in Aden, the perfume factory at Maala, and a foam rubber factory at Sheikh Othman. The factories are 50 per cent state owned, 40 per cent private, and 10 per cent is controlled by the Union. Such participation ensures some financial gain to the Union as well as helping to expand female employment.

These large-scale activities have been supplemented by a countrywide programme aimed at involving the more traditional, house-bound women in some kind of economic activity. Handicrafts have been a special focus here, and straw weaving, pottery and rug making co-operatives have been set up; this is partly, in the case of the poorer women, to help them maximise their own resources by teaching them how to recycle materials that would otherwise be wasted. The Union is keen to involve women who are still subject to *purdah* restrictions in income-generating work that they can do at home in the hope that this might provide some measure of economic independence. The emphasis on handicrafts as an activity aimed at women has certain advantages but there are also some dangers: it may channel women into areas of low productivity and low remuneration where effort is not matched by reward and where, moreover, their economic contribution remains low.

The Women's Union is the forum for debating policy issues relating to women; its cadres are consulted over new legislation and are, at least in theory, encouraged to take an active part in extending the provisions of existing laws and eradicating anomalies. Apart from these activities, the Women's Union carries out a number of pastoral functions. Its members arbitrate in divorce proceedings, acting as marriage counsellors, usually via the Popular Defence Councils, and helping to sort out problems arising over custody of children. They try to ensure that marriages conform to the Family Law's statutes regarding consent and age of marriage, and they carry out a variety of different kinds of welfare work; these range from helping on campaigns to promote breastfeeding instead of using powdered milk, to rehabilitating prostitutes. However, the GUYW does not see itself as a feminist organisation in the sense of existing principally to further the interests of women *per se*; rather it acts as part of the state's political apparatus and as such its function is to implement government policies which affect women. Thus, measures which could be taken to improve the position of women are considered in the context of other longer-term objectives.

NOTES

1) This account has been constructed on the basis of interviews with prominent officials of the Women's Union and other women active in these societies and during the Independence struggle. See Molyneux (1980) for the account by Women's Union officials.

CHAPTER II

EDUCATION

The third area of government policy which can be expected to yield changes in the position of women is that of education. Along with women's entry into employment, education is seen by the government as a vital pre-condition for women's emancipation and as the main weapon in the ideological struggle against what is generally termed "traditionalism". But as with the entry of women into economic activity, so with the spread of education; there are pressing material reasons for this to be encouraged which reinforce the ideological commitment. The country urgently requires educated personnel to fulfil its development plans and has for this reason pursued a policy of rapid expansion in formal educational facilities for both boys and girls.

In education as in other areas, Democratic Yemen faces a serious shortage of resources. At Independence approximately 90 per cent of the population were illiterate and there were less than 400 schools in the whole country; all but 60 of these were primary schools. Most of these catered for boys, although as we will see in more detail later, by 1967 girls made up 25.7 per cent of the total school population of 64,202. The majority of pre-Independence schools fell into two main types, the *kuttabs* or independent schools and the *mailamats* or religious schools which were normally attached to the mosques. A minority fell into a third category, namely those set up by the British Government after 1948. In 1968 a decree was passed nationalising most of the private schools and bringing all educational establishments under state control. The government endorsed the principle of free education for all children of school age and a programme to extend the number of schools in existence was drawn up. As can be seen from table 1, by 1977 the number of schools had more

Table 1: Statistical indicators of formal education 1966/67 – 1976/77

	Number of Schools			Enrolments			Participation rate as a % of relevant age group		
	Primary	Prepar.	Secondary	Primary	Prepar.	Secondary	Primary	Prepar.	Secondary
1966/67	329	53	7	49,928	11,343	2,992	–	–	–
1970/71	844	59	8	134,884	13,658	3,023	51.0	15.0	4.2
1973/74	1,026	105	19	183,744	23,245	6,933	63.6	23.4	8.8
1974/75	963	151		196,466	30,474	7,915	66.0	29.8	9.7
1975/76	962	191	21	203,617	34,348	9,767	66.5	32.7	11.7
1976/77	976	326	25	206,358	43,410	10,946	65.4	40.1	12.8

Primary and Preparatory Schools are being combined into one level in the new Unity schools scheme.

Source: World Bank (1979).

than trebled, reaching a total of 1,327. Of these, 74 per cent are primary schools although there has been some expansion at other levels as well. This was especially so at the intermediate level which shows a sixfold increase over previous figures.[1] The relatively rapid increase in the number of schools was in part due to the success of self-help schemes in which village communities provided volunteer labour. Funds for these projects were also raised by contributions from emigrant workers. Government expenditure also reflects the importance accorded to education: according to government figures, in the fiscal year 1967/68 only 9.7 per cent of the general budget was allocated to education. By 1975/76 the percentage had increased by 74 per cent to 16.9.

The figures also show that the number of pupils enrolled in schools increased fourfold from a total of 64,263 in 1966 to 260,714 a decade later, with most of the increased intake at primary level. As table 2 below shows the participation rate for both boys and girls has increased substantially since 1960 in both primary and secondary schools, although in the former the girls' rate of enrolment is still just over half that of the boys'.[2]

Table 2: Number enrolled in school as a percentage of age group

		Primary				Secondary*	
Total		Males		Females		Total	
1960	1977	1960	1977	1960	1977	1960	1977
17	77	20	99	5	54	5	26

* Disaggregated figures are not provided.
Source: World Bank (1980).

In addition to the expansion of conventional educational establishments, some schools have been reserved by the government for the children of the Bedouin in an attempt to promote the settlement of the nomadic tribal communities and their integration into the wider society. There are 23 primary Bedouin schools with 27,572 pupils, 3,552 of which are girls; 10 intermediate schools with 1,060 pupils, only 15 of which are girls; and three secondary schools with 145 pupils, all of whom are boys. A few of these Bedouin schools were built in the pre-Independence period by the British Government but they have since been added to and the existing ones have been converted to meet the aims of the present scheme. Most of these establishments are boarding schools which take children from the age of 6 or 7 until they are 15, but some resistance by families to releasing their children, especially their daughters, from useful activity in the home has been encountered. In some areas the government has had to pay the parents a small compensatory sum for the loss of the child's labour in order to help overcome this initial reluctance. Once in the schools the children are taught a variety of subjects and skills including the martial arts. Children from these schools can be seen in military parades equipped with their uniforms and guns, forming a corps of junior militia men and women, many of whom will later pass into the armed forces.

Finally, for pre-school children in the urban areas the government has inaugurated a programme to build what are called "kindergartens" with a view to relieving the burden of child-care on the working mother. Yet these are not nurseries. Children are normally accepted only from the age of 5, but if the mother is a wage-earner children a year younger are considered. In 1977 there were 17 such establishments with a total enrolment of 3,881 children of whom 2,123 were boys and 1,758 girls.[3] The schools provide a free meal a day and, where resources permit, transport for outlying pupils. In these schools children are encouraged to do craftwork, singing, drama, and political history as well as to learn how to read and write. In addition to the building of more kindergartens in urban areas, future housing plans envisage nurseries in the building complexes for residents, although these will not offer any educational training. There are as yet no nursery schools to cater to the under-fives, although some are planned for location in the larger industrial enterprises with a high concentration of women workers.

In higher education there has been a similar expansion in universities, teacher training colleges, vocational centres and technical institutes. In 1976 there were 24 colleges of higher education (including the different faculties of Aden University) and these claimed between them some 5,000 students. About 1,200 of these are accounted for by the University (a fourfold increase over figures for 1970) and about 500 by the Technical Institute in Maala. The rest were distributed in colleges specialising in such areas as teacher training, medicine and agriculture.

Accompanying this expansion of educational facilities, there has been a qualitative change in the education system brought about by a reorientation of Democratic Yemen's educational policy. The guidelines for this policy were laid down in the first Education Conference in 1975 and these entailed a major reorganisation of both the structure of teaching and of the syllabi. The tripartite division of schooling into six years of primary, three years of intermediary and three years of secondary found in many Arab countries was to be replaced by a two-tier primary/secondary system of eight years and six years respectively which abolished the intermediate level altogether.[4] This system, similar to that found in the German Democratic Republic, is being put into practice in the new "Unity" schools which have been spreading throughout the country since 1976.

The syllabi have also undergone a number of important changes. First, they were transformed in order more closely to "meet the demands of the economy". This has meant that a greater emphasis has been placed on vocational training in schools. In the rural areas, in particular, training is given to promote the acquisition of skills which will be of practical advantage to the local economy. Changes have also been made in order "to teach the principles of scientific socialism" and to "form the new Yemeni personality". Textbooks now include works on historical materialism, and some of the writings of Marx, Engels, Lenin and even Krupskay are listed as required reading in some courses. Religious instruction is also provided, and the Koran taught in such a way as to suggest points of comparison between socialism and Islam. The new curricula are taught where possible with the most up-to-date textbooks and teaching methods. An attempt has also been made to introduce the new maths into some schools, although finding teachers able to teach it has proved difficult and as elsewhere, parents have had problems in helping their children with homework. At the

25

same time such subjects as the music and literature of the Yemens, handicrafts and physical training, have been extensively introduced in order to "narrow the gap between school and life".

The shortage of qualified teaching staff is still a major problem. Many of the existing personnel (80 per cent of 9,553 *in toto*, according to one report) are underqualified and are further disadvantaged by the extra demands of curriculum changes. At the higher levels almost half of the staff are non-nationals, mostly Indians, Arabs and some Eastern Europeans. The majority have tended to come from India, since its main foreign language is English and a significant proportion of Democratic Yemen's higher education courses are taught in English. From Democratic Yemen's point of view, recruiting non-nationals has major drawbacks; they cannot always attract the best teachers or the ones most sympathetic to their politics and curricula; and in order to attract any teachers at all, internationally competitive salaries have to be paid, at levels sometimes four times the local salary. While this creates marked divisions and opens up the possibility of resentment between local and foreign teaching staff, it also represents a drain on the country's resources because of the high salaries in convertible currency that these foreigners command.

1. Literacy

The expansion and restructuring of formal education has been accompanied by a mass adult literacy campaign conducted between the years 1973 and 1976, in order to eliminate high levels of illiteracy. As illustrated by table 3 below, the most

Table 3: Population by sex and educational status (for persons over 10 years of age), 1973

	Female	%	Male	%	Total	%
Urban population,	163,522		188,577		352,099	
of which illiterates	130,456	79.8	72,423	38.4	202,879	57.6
Rural population,	311,279		256,858		568,137	
of which illiterates	298,985	96.0	136,935	53.6	435,920	76.7
Nomads,	52,965		51,188		104,153	
of which illiterates	52,606	99.3	44,819	87.5	97,425	93.5
Total,	527,766		496,623		1,024,389	
of which illiterates	482,047	91.3	254,177	51.2	736,224	71.9

Source: World Bank (1979).

disadvantaged groups were women and nomads with illiteracy rates of 91.3 per cent and 93.5 per cent respectively. Urban males were the most privileged in this respect with a 36.4 per cent illiteracy rate over-all.

Although attempts to promote literacy formed an integral part of government educational policy from 1968, it was not until 1973, with the launching of the campaign, that serious efforts were made to commit substantial resources at the national level. For the first time centres for co-ordinating literacy programmes were established in all six governorates. Classes were made compulsory for illiterate wage-earners and a government decree made literacy a requirement of all state employees. In addition, it was incumbent upon employers to allocate at least one hour of each working day for teaching to take place. The campaign was directed at both men and women, although since it tended to be organised at the place of work special classes had to be arranged for women confined to their homes. More than twice as many women as men responded to the campaign, a fact that reflected the considerably higher rate of female illiteracy. The campaign was given nationwide publicity and various types of incentives were introduced for qualified literates. These included increased job opportunities and even wage increments for some workers; three Yemeni Dinars per month was the usual incentive for attending classes and five Yemeni Dinars per month for passing the test. (An unskilled worker earns between 16 YD and 25 YD per month.) In some factories literacy came to be a condition of employment.

Although the number of certificate holders in the three years of the campaign reached nearly 34,000, the project was less successful than had been hoped. One unpublished official report claims that by the end of 1976 a total of 188,421 people had enrolled in literacy classes. Of these 33,957 or 18 per cent passed their literacy tests, although it must be assumed that at the time of the survey others who later passed were still waiting to do so. As can be seen from table 4 below, of those who passed by this date 15,286 were men and 18,671 were women. It is worth noting that in

Table 4:   Number of literacy certificate holders

	Male	Female	Total	Females as % of total
1973/74	3,503	1,786	5,289	33.8
1974/75	4,831	5,915	10,746	55.0
1975/76	6,952	10,970	17,922	61.2
Total	15,286	18,671	33,957	55.0

Source: General Office for Eradicating Illiteracy and Promoting Adult Education (1977).

These figures for those who enrolled but did not graduate are higher than those given by the World Bank study on pages 50 and 180 of the 1979 report. World Bank (1980).

the first year of the campaign nearly three times as many men as women graduated, in the second year women represented a slight majority over men and in the third year women were in a substantial majority with over a third more women than men graduates.

Among the main problems encountered by the government was a high drop-out rate of 40 per cent from the classes. Another was the unavailability of qualified teachers; as most of these had been absorbed into formal education, there was an over-reliance on poorly trained volunteers who often had no teaching experience whatsoever and some of whom were barely literate themselves. The campaign had been modelled on the successful Cuban experience in eradicating illiteracy, but the significant difference between the two countries was that the general level of education in Cuba was much higher to begin with than in Democratic Yemen. In 1960 Cuba had only a 32 per cent illiteracy rate, whereas in 1979 Democratic Yemen had a rate of over 90 per cent. Moreover, the educational level of the Cuban volunteers was probably much higher than in Democratic Yemen. According to the World Bank Report the over-all literacy rate in Democratic Yemen by 1975 was still only 13 per cent (World Bank, 1980).

2. Girls' education

The Constitutional commitment to democratise education by making it freely available to all citizens of Democratic Yemen signified a fundamental change in the prospects for girls' education. Although there is nothing in Islam prohibiting the education of women, only a handful of schools accepted girls prior to 1967. These were mainly at primary level, although in Aden there existed a few secondary schools for girls, some of which were set up by the British Government. But over-all, scant provision for female education had been made by the colonial state. As one British report made clear, boys were to be given priority over girls because local customs restricted the possibility of educated women being employed and it was therefore pointless to undertake more than a minimum commitment in this area (Adenisation Committee, 1959). By contrast, current government policy is actively to encourage female education. There are three main reasons for this. The first is to develop the skill potential of the female labour force and to encourage women's entry into employment. The second is to educate women so as to better contribute to the education of their children. The third is to advance the education of women as one of the main weapons in the struggle against tradition and for greater equality between the sexes.

Most educational institutions in Democratic Yemen are open to both sexes although some single-sex establishments which pre-date Independence survive.[5] In general Democratic Yemen has opted for co-education despite both internal and external opposition. While the government has stood its ground in part because of a commitment to the principle of desegregation, economic imperatives have also been a factor. The extreme scarcity of resources does not permit unnecessary duplication of teachers' time and school facilities (see Democratic Yemen, Ministry of Education, 1976).

The discrepancies in the published and unpublished statistics on education make rigorous analysis impossible, but all figures show that there has been a substantial increase in female participation since Independence. According to the World Bank figures given in table 2, at primary level the female enrolment rate (i.e. the number enrolled in school as a percentage of the age group) increased from 5 per cent in 1960 to 54 per cent in 1977. At the same time the equivalent figure for boys rose to 99 per cent by 1977, indicating a 20 per cent increase on the 1960 figures. Although these figures show dramatic increases and may overstate the real situation, all the available statistics testify to a gradual reduction in the sexual imbalance and a substantial increase in female participation. None the less, the sexual asymmetry remains significant. This is even clearer if we look at the numerical increase. In 1966/67 according to table 5, only 13,158 girls were represented in the three school

Table 5: Statistical indicators of formal education

| | Enrolments by sex | | | | | |
| | Primary | | Preparatory | | Secondary | |
	Male	Female	Male	Female	Male	Female
1966/67	39,762	10,166	8,897	2,685	2,446	546
1970/71	107,925	26,959	10,994	2,664	2,344	679
1973/74	136,577	47,167	18,537	4,708	5,509	1,424
1974/75	136,855	59,611	24,007	6,397	6,324	1,591
1975/76	135,653	67,964	26,623	7,725	7,568	2,199
1976/77	134,827	71,531	32,628	10,782	8,620	2,326

Source: World Bank (1979).

levels — primary, preparatory and secondary. Ten years later the figure had increased sixfold to 84,639. During the same period the number of boys in school had more than trebled to reach 176,075, or twice that of girls. In terms of the total school population, girls therefore made up only 32 per cent of the students in 1976/77 thereby increasing their share by about 12 per cent over the 10 years since 1967. As with boys most girls are concentrated in primary school and this is where the most significant increase in female enrolment has taken place. Table 5 shows that whereas the intake of boys at primary level trebled, that of girls increased sevenfold. At preparatory and secondary levels the rate of increase is more evenly distributed. At both these levels the number of boys increased three and a half times in each case, whereas that of girls increased four and a half times and four times respectively. By 1977 girls' enrolment was about one-third that of boys at preparatory level and about one-quarter that of boys at secondary. According to unpublished Ministry of Education figures for 1976, the female enrolment rate at primary level was only 22.6 per cent, at preparatory 9.9 per cent and at secondary 2.7 per cent. These figures, as mentioned above, are lower than those given by the World Bank (q.v., p. 34). Thus while the number of girls in schools has risen faster than that of boys, it still represents a low over-all participation rate. This low enrolment rate is compounded by a higher drop-out rate among girls. According to some official estimates the drop-out rate from school is 44 per cent; of this 27 per cent is accounted for by girls.

Low female participation therefore remains a central problem and a serious limit on women's later employment opportunities. One factor explaining this differential is that it is not yet compulsory to educate girls whereas it is so to educate boys. Moreover, whereas the government aims at 100 per cent enrolment of boys over the next decade, it has set its target at 80 per cent for girls. This may be interpreted as reflecting either bias or realism, but the problem of unequal participation, found in so many Third World countries, has found no simple short-term solution. It derives from a complex combination of factors both material and ideological, and while these are susceptible to change, this will only come slowly in the absence of a deliberate and well planned strategy to accelerate it. Some indication of the underlying tensions in this area is provided by a report of an enquiry into the causes of girls low level of attendance at schools in the second governorate (see Education Research Centre, 1976). The major finding of this enquiry was that parental resistance to educating their daughters accounted for a significant percentage of female absentees. According to the report this resistance was motivated primarily by economic considerations and in most cases by extreme poverty. Girls were kept away from school, not because parents disapproved of educating girls on principle, but rather because they were needed at home to help their mothers with domestic chores, mind the younger children, work in the fields or tend the herds. But a further rationalisation for not educating girls was also advanced, namely that since girls were destined for marriage and not for paid work the family's investment in an education would be unlikely to reap them any rewards. While boys could reasonably be expected to use their education by taking up paid employment and thereby become a financial asset to the family, girls were unlikely to do so and were, said to be, "better at home". In the words of the report: "the common customs do not allow girls to work as boys do, and they compel them to marry early".

However, some of the survey's findings were more encouraging. Where attitudes to female education are concerned it appeared that the cultural and ideological resistance to girls' education was less than had been expected. Most of the men interviewed accepted the beneficial effects of female education, and teachers unanimously supported the principle of educating girls even if there were disagreements as to how far up the educational ladder this should be pursued. Significantly, all the women teachers thought that girls should be encouraged to reach university level, whilst their male colleagues considered secondary education sufficient. All teachers supported compulsory education for girls and approved the provisions of the Education Labour laws which prohibit schoolchildren from working in school hours. However, what the survey indicates is that the low participation rates of girls cannot be remedied until the sexual division of labour in the society at large is changed with a corresponding change in attitudes towards women's place in society. Until families are convinced that it is worthwhile to release girls from the domestic economy into schooling, there will persist a tendency for them to be kept at home working for their families and being encouraged to see marriage as their sole destiny.

On the basis of its findings the survey recommended financial compensation for families with daughters at school, a measure which found considerable support among the families interviewed. It also recommended that the requirement to wear school uniforms be dropped as poor families could not afford to buy them; that crèches be provided in order to release young girls from having to look after their younger brothers and sisters; and that sewing and typing pools be set up both to train the daughters and to provide families with ways of earning extra income to help support the loss of their daughter's labour. Positive as some of these recommendations might have seemed, they pre-supposed a level of state support which is unlikely in the restricted economic conditions Democratic Yemen finds itself in.

The disparity between male and female participation rates is also found in higher education where less than 25 per cent of the students at the university are women, and an even smaller percentage of technical college enrolments are by women. On the basis of the figures in table 6 below, women make up only 19.5 per cent of students in the listed vocational training institutions. There are no statistics available on the pre-revolutionary period, but since there was little provision for such training

Table 6: Enrolment in vocational training
institutions, 1975–76

Type of institution	Total	Male	Female
Higher college	789	597	192
Agriculture college	97	84	13
College of administration	237	190	47
College of engineering	76	69	7
Technical institute	494	450	44
Teacher training	794	563	231
General secondary commercial and agriculture	361	290	71
Professional institute	1,151	974	177
Medical college	63	49	14
Total	4,062	3,266	796

Source: Democratic Yemen, Central Statistical Organisation (1976).

and even less for women, we can assume that this figure, although low, represents a substantial advance since Independence. As in many other countries women have gravitated towards professions such as teaching and have barely penetrated those which are conventionally associated with "men's" skills, such as engineering. Although these rates of participation are still low, they would be even lower if it were not for a measure of positive discrimination adopted by some colleges. This allows women to gain admission with lower qualifications than men. However women seem to do comparatively better in higher education than they do at the lower levels.

31

Examination results for Aden University colleges show no significant sexual disparity between the pass rates of men and women. Indeed women sometimes do better than men; in three out of six degrees for which information is available (science, literature and agricultural studies) the over-all pass rate for women was higher than for the male students.

Table 7:   Examination results for colleges of Aden
               University, 1976–77

Course	Sex	Registered	% Pass
Higher College of Education (1st/5th Governorates)			
Diploma: Literature	M	27	85.2
	F	36	77.8
Diploma: Sciences	M	10	80.0
	F	13	84.6
Bachelor: Literature	M	34	85.3
	F	17	88.2
Bachelor: Sciences	M	14	78.6
	F	3	100.0
Nasser College of Agricultural Sciences			
Agriculture	M	12	83.3
	F	7	100.0
College of Economics and Administration	M	20	100.0
	F	6	100.0

Source: Ketab al-Ahsa al-Tarbawi al Sanawi L-Am, 1976–77 (Democratic Yemen, Ministry of Education, unpublished).

NOTES

1) However, of the pupils who attended primary school only about 50 per cent proceeded to intermediate level and of those who completed the intermediate stage only about 20 per cent reached secondary level (Ministry of Education figures, 1977, unpublished).
2) There is a considerable discrepancy between the figures given in tables 1 and 2, although they provide an indication of the changes which have taken place and their direction.
3) Ketab al-Ahsa al-Tarbawi al Sanawi L-Am, 1976-77 (Annual Educational Statistics, Ministry of Education, 1977).
4) According to official sources the introduction of this system in Democratic Yemen was also influenced partly by the Sudanese model.
5) One headmistress, however, said that in her experience girls did significantly better in single sex schools.

CHAPTER III

EMPLOYMENT

As in other areas, there has been substantial progress in improving employment opportunities for women since the pre-Independence period, although in the last decade of colonial rule gradual changes were coming into effect in Aden itself. Before this, however, during the first half of the 1950s, very few women appear to have entered employment even in Aden and there were only limited kinds of wage work available to them (see Aden Colony, 1955). This was compounded by the fact that women of working age were far outnumbered in Aden by men as single male migrants absorbed a high proportion of the jobs that became available as the port economy expanded.

As with the statistics on education, those on employment are inconsistent and are also incomplete. These problems are compounded by shifting usages of definitional categories such as labour force, employment and economically active population. In the absence of the original methodological guidelines it has not been possible to reclassify the data, so they are presented here as given in the original texts, except in the few instances where the meaning is clear in the original and can be easily redefined.

In the pre-Independence period, the only employment information available is on Aden, so the data on employment in the city and its suburbs will be presented here. In 1955, according to the population census, of a total population of the city of Aden and its suburbs of 136,666, 68.8 per cent (94,149) were male and 31.1 per cent (42,517) were female. The 1955 Aden census in fact understates the sexual imbalance among adults since the male-female ratio is much more equal among children and since it excludes the thousands of British servicemen in the city, and the many sailors who would be there at any one time. But the imbalances recorded for 1955 diminished somewhat in the following decade as more women from what was formerly known as North Yemen or the Adeni hinterland came to stay with their menfolk in the city.[1]

Official reports on the 1950s suggest that for Adeni Arab women the only job openings at this time were in nursing, midwifery or other areas of the health service, and that Somali women, worked as *ayahs* (child-minders) and cleaners of coffee and incense; the latter worked a ten-hour day, six days a week, for between 3 and 5 shillings a day earned on a piecework basis. There is evidence to suggest that there was some employment of women in small workshops, since the 1956 figures for Aden give a total of 686 women in employment (out of a total economically active male and female population of 28,387). Of these 686 women, 135 were in government and other services, and 551 in industry. There also seems to have been some demand by women for employment since the 1955 Population Census remarks that female unemployment is high at between 5 and 21 per cent in different parts of Aden. This reportedly high unemployment contrasts with a situation of full or near-full employment for men. This high unemployment rate among women is however not confirmed by the Employment Exchange where very few women registered. This

35

apparent inconsistency might be explained by the fact that women were interested in finding work, but could not yet bring themselves to go to the public authorities in order to obtain it.

By 1958 the number of women registered in Aden as employed had risen to 818 or 2.3 per cent of the total number of 35,191 males and females in employment: of these, 41 women worked in the port, 237 in government and other services, and 540 in industry. A government report for the period records that educated women had begun to register at the Employment Exchange, and in 1961 a special women's section of the Exchange was opened. In 1962, the authorities set up a Domestic Training School to train Arab women in domestic service, and by the end of 1963, 120 women had graduated from this body. The data nearest Independence are for 1965 and they record that out of a total of 63,975 in employment, 1,381 were women (see Democratic Yemen, Department of Labour and Welfare, 1965). Of these, 20 worked in the port, 673 in industry, 319 in retail and wholesale enterprises, 351 in government and other services, and 18 in other positions. The official report indicates that the Employment Exchange was helping women to find work "as clerks, telephonists, shop assistants or in other unskilled occupations". The trend indicated by these official reports is therefore clearly one of a gradual increase in female employment opportunities, and there is reason to believe that the figures given in the Department of Labour and Welfare Reports understate the real situation. The 1955 Population Census gives a figure for total employment of 51,301, far higher than other statistics for the period (the Department of Labour and Welfare reports 28,387 for 1956), and this discrepancy recurs in the data on women: the census gives female employment at 1,969, three times higher than comparable government data and 9 per cent of the total adult female population in Aden, where adult is defined as over 21 years of age (Aden Colony, 1955, p. 29). This discrepancy can be explained as a result of the somewhat broader definition of employment used by the 1955 Population Census, which probably included some categories of unpaid family labour and own-account workers.

Since Independence there has been a drive to increase the participation of women in the labour force and to alter the skill structure of employed women. Two main factors have contributed to this. First, there is the over-all programme of economic development, embodied in the 1971-74 Three-Year Plan. After the *negative* GNP growth rates of 10 to 15 per cent immediately following Independence, GNP was rising at around 8 per cent per annum by 1977 (World Bank, 1979). During the first decade after Independence there took place a comprehensive transformation of all sectors of the economy by the state: agrarian reform has involved the establishment of about 40 state farms and an equal number of state-financed collectives; industrial development has been promoted by state support; import and export trade has been brought under state control; and, whilst many private shops remain, a new state retail system has also come into existence alongside them. The demand for labour has therefore increased substantially, especially in the industrial and service sectors of the urban economy. Second, Democratic Yemen suffers from an acute labour shortage in certain sectors and from a problem of underutilisation of existing labour supplies. Whilst reflecting an underlying lack of skills, this has been compounded by the effects of successive decades of emigration. Although this was stopped in 1973, up to 300,000 citizens of Democratic Yemen work abroad, many of them in the oil-producing states where wages are much higher. With approximately one out of three able-bodied men between the ages of 15-34 still living abroad, the demand for

36

women in employment as a result of the combination of a small population and emigration remains high (see World Bank, 1979). Despite the substantial reduction in open unemployment since 1967 shown by table 8 below, more than half of the labour potential of the country is not in the active labour market, and many of those who are not economically active are women.

Table 8:   Population, manpower and labour force
           (in thousands)

	1969	1973	1976
Total population	1,486	1,712	1,805
of which less than 12 years old	575	648	713
over 65 years old	54	62	67
migrants (adults and children)	70	122	125
Working age population	787	880	900
of which incapables	68	80	88
Manpower potential	719	800	812
of which not seeking jobs	408	441	396
Total labour force	311	359	416
of which unemployed	47	36	17

Source: World Bank (1979).

The State has taken active steps to encourage women to enter the labour force. Key levers have been education, vocational training programmes, and the labour exchanges. This emphasis on women's entry into social production, i.e. work outside the home, not only reflects the objective needs of the economy for women's labour, but is also seen as the main part of the struggle to help women to emancipate themselves from traditional forms of subordination through acquiring a measure of economic independence. Some indication of the success of the government's attempt to mobilise urban women into economic activity can be gained from the increasing numbers of female job applications processed through the Aden labour exchanges.

Following a pattern common to most countries, far fewer women than men make themselves available for employment by registering at labour exchanges or actively seeking work, and this is despite the fact that there are many more women without jobs than men. The Ministry of Labour figures in table 9 show that the number of men who registered for employment in 1976 (4,230) was three times that of the number of women (1,553). However, whereas the number of men seeking jobs had declined since 1967 when it stood at 7,076, the number of women jobseekers shows an increase of nearly two and a half times over the 1967 figure. In 1967 only 604 women were

37

Table 9: Registration of appointments and unemployment
in the First Governorate for 9.3.1967 to 31.12.1976

Years	Unemployed		Appointed		Registered	
	Females	Males	Females	Males	Females	Males
March 1967	523	5,507	81	1,569	604	7,076
1968	527	4,769	125	1,657	652	6,426
1969	357	1,341	122	1,306	479	2,647
1970	441	2,323	123	1,559	564	3,882
1971	1,007	2,601	256	2,334	1,263	4,935
1972	553	2,026	227	1,938	780	3,964
1973	1,863	5,953	121	1,845	1,984	7,789
1974	2,510	2,373	356	3,660	2,866	6,033
1975	1,085	119	963	4,736	2,048	4,855
1976	312	–	1,241	4,751	1,553	4,230

Source: Based on data provided by the Ministry of Labour and Civil Service.

registered as seeking jobs, but in 1976 the number had risen to 1,553. Yet, despite the increased availability of women between 1967 and 1976, many more men were able to find jobs than women over this period. Thus the supply of female labour apparently exceeded demand. More encouraging are the 1976 figures which show that the percentage of women who attained employment from labour exchanges had reached its highest-ever level of 80 per cent, albeit in a year when virtually no men remained on the books without jobs.

1. Economic activity of women

There are a variety of different and contradictory sources on the distribution of the labour force by sex and industry so the data presented here must be regarded as approximate. The economically active population was reported by the 1973 Population Census to be 409,700 (or 26 per cent of the total population) and the World Bank (1980) estimates an annual increase of 1.3 per cent over the 1970-1980 period. The relatively young age of the population helps to account for this low figure. According to the 1973 Population Census nearly one out of every five persons was under 5 years of age and roughly half of the population was under 15 years old. Table 10 shows the distribution of employment by sex and industry, according to 1973 figures.

Table 10: Employment by sex and industry in Democratic Yemen, 1973
(in per cent)

Industry	Total	Male	Female
Agriculture, hunting, live-stock, fishing	52.0	44.6	87.2
Mining and quarrying	0.6	0.8	–
Manufacturing	4.5	4.7	3.6
Electricity, gas and water	0.9	1.1	0.1
Construction	4.8	5.8	–
Transport, storage and communications	4.2	5.0	0.1
Finance, insurance and business services	0.1	0.2	0.1
Wholesale and retail trade and restaurants	8.0	9.5	0.4
Community, social and personal services	24.9	28.3	8.5
Total	100.00	100.00	100.00
Number	319,686	265,138	54,548

Source: Democratic Yemen, Central Planning Commission (1974).

The data in table 10 show that in 1973 more than half of those in employment were concentrated in agriculture, 11 per cent were in the secondary sector, 4.5 per cent in manufacturing and 4.8 per cent in construction. The service sector employed 37 per cent of the total (see UN ECWA, 1980). The World Bank Report, however, tells a different story. According to its 1980 Report, in 1978, 60 per cent of the economically active population of Democratic Yemen was concentrated in agriculture, 21 per cent in industry and 19 per cent in services. This shows a decrease of 10 per cent over 1960 figures in agriculture and an increase of 6 and 4 per cent respectively in industry and services. Both sets of statistics do agree however that there has been a decline in agriculture's hold over the population and a rise in both secondary and tertiary sector employment.

On the basis of the 1973 figures, women made up 19 per cent of those registered as economically active, and according to the 1980 World Bank Report, this had risen slightly to approximately 20 per cent by 1980. Low though this may appear, it is far higher than comparable figures in many other Muslim countries, although all such figures tend to underestimate the real female labour force participation in the informal sector and in agriculture. Table 11 shows that for 1976, of a total female population of 880,301, 33,571 are classified as unpaid workers which is nearly twice as many as those who are paid employees.

Table 11: Estimated population of the Republic for the
year 1976 distributed by sex and employment status

Employment status	Female	Male
Less than 7 years old	223,035	231,516
Employer	296	18,625
Own-account workers	20,832	95,644
Employee	6,014	149,365
Unpaid worker	33,571	34,699
Unemployed	17,562	61,659
Not at work and not seeking work	522,954	237,952
Unable to work	56,037	33,041
Total	880,301	862,502

Total population of Democratic Yemen, 1976: 1,742,803.

Source: Democratic Yemen, Central Statistical Organisation (provisional estimate).

As far as the over-all distribution of women in the employment structure is concerned, no reliable figures are available and information is scattered and fragmentary. Table 10 shows the preponderant hold of agriculture on female employment, with 87.2 per cent of the total in this sector and only one-sixth of the female active labour force engaged in urban occupations. After agriculture the largest number of women (8.5 per cent) are employed in what are termed "community, social and personal services" and manufacturing (3.6 per cent). These categories unfortunately tell us more about the activities from which women are virtually excluded — mining, construction, trade, transport and finance — than about precisely where they are employed, and what work they do.

2. Agriculture

As we have seen, agriculture is the most important sector as far as employment is concerned and accounts for more than half of the total labour force. There are no available figures on what percentage of the agricultural labour force *per se* is female but in category 1 of the government's classification system which includes agriculture along with hunting and fishing, 52,150 women are economically active, comprising 40 per cent of all those in this category,[2] and nearly 80 per cent of all economically active women. Since women have for a long time participated in agricultural production, the question is not how far they have entered employment but how far their position within the division of labour has altered. The rural training schemes have enabled some women to acquire skills they did not have access to before, but the level of skill, like the

40

level of literacy, is still very low among rural women and it will take a long time for this to change. In the co-operatives, where, with few exceptions only the "heads" of families are entitled to membership, a very small percentage of women are represented, and on the state farms it is only a handful of women who play a role in decision-making procedures.

3. The urban sector

Although only between one-fifth and one-sixth of the female labour force is found in urban occupations, the more noticeable changes in women's participation have come about in the urban sector where women form 7 per cent of urban employees. This is low by comparison with the male participation rate, but women's jobs in this sector have expanded considerably in the last decade, at the same time as there has been a substantial change in the kinds of jobs open to them. Women have begun to enter two types of employment previously closed to them: the first is into jobs which in many countries are performed almost entirely by women but which in Democratic Yemen as in other Muslim countries were traditionally monopolised by men; the second is into jobs which are conventionally associated with male labour both inside and outside Democratic Yemen, but where women are now entering in small numbers. Examples of the former include nursing, shop assistants, clerical work and domestic service; and examples of the latter include technical and mechanical work, and most of the professions.

The entry of women into the first type of employment has been far more substantial than into the second, although men still predominate in all the occupations mentioned above.[3] This is slowly changing however, partly because more women are being trained in these areas, and partly because as some jobs become increasingly identified with female employment, there is a tendency for men to seek either more senior posts or alternative employment. It is now government policy to encourage women to take the place of men as sales staff, nurses, secretaries and typists. According to the Ministry of Trade, 60 per cent of the staff in government shops are now women. There are also several hundred women working as secretaries and typists although the more important white collar jobs are still predominantly held by men.[4]

The expansion of health and educational services has provided the largest number of employment opportunities for women in both the categories above and this is reflected in the steady expansion of the number of women recruited over the years since 1971. However, in medicine as in education, women have only penetrated the higher echelons in small numbers. There are as yet very few female instructors at post-graduate level, and only 10 women doctors out of a total of 156. Moreover, as can be seen from table 12, fewer women are being trained in medicine even at middle range levels: at the Institute of Health and Manpower Development, of the 204 graduates only 42 or 20 per cent were women, despite the Institute's 50 per cent female student target. These female graduates tended to be concentrated in midwifery and medical assistantships — jobs at the lower end of the pay scale. Most women in medicine are either para-medicals or nurses and in these areas they are still in the minority even if this is a sizeable one. In 1975, 40 per cent of para-medicals were women and this is the occupation with the largest concentration of women in the medical profession.

41

Table 12:   Graduates of the Institutes of Health and Manpower
            Development, 1977-78

	Male	Female	Total	Females as % of total
Professional nursing	28	4	32	12.5
Practical nursing	40	7	47	14.8
Medical assistants	35	–	35	0
Pharmacy technicans	13	2	15	13.3
Assistant pharmacy technicians	–	–	–	–
Health inspectors	9	–	9	0
Assistant radiographers	13	–	13	0
Assistant laboratory technicians	24	–	24	0
Nurse/midwife	–	7	7	100
Community nurse/ midwife	–	22	22	100
	162	42	204	20.5

Source: Democratic Yemen Director of Health Statistics, Ministry of Health (1978)
         cited in Democratic Yemen, MCH Services (1979).

Many women have been absorbed into teaching, another area previously monopolised by men. School teaching in many countries is conventionally associated with high female employment, particularly at primary level. Yet in Democratic Yemen men still predominate over women at all levels; of the 9,550 school teachers only 26 per cent are women (1976-77). As table 13 shows, even at primary level men far outnumber women; in 1977 there were 6,598 male primary school teachers compared with only 2,420 females.

This preponderance of men not only reflects the shortage of women teachers but also the fact that teaching is still regarded as a prestige occupation even at primary level, and therefore continues to attract men.

By contrast, the 17 kindergartens are staffed almost entirely by women, and the Head of the Kindergarten Planning Board affirmed her belief that women were best suited to looking after small children. She did, however, concede that the few men employed in the kindergartens were excellent at their jobs. Over-all, despite the relatively small number of women in the teaching profession compared with that of men, the number of women recruited has steadily grown since 1970, although at a slower pace than male recruitment. Table 14 shows a promising reversal of the trend for more men than women to apply for training; in 1977 the number of women students for the first time exceeded that of men, with a substantial difference in favour of women. This could indicate the direction of change in Democratic Yemen, involving

Table 13: Number of teachers, 1966–77

Year	Primary		Preparatory		Secondary	
	Male	Female	Male	Female	Male	Female
1966-67	1,378	367	–	–	116	49
1970-71*	4,316		630		139	
1973-74	4,831	1,524	722	227	293	87
1974-75	4,885	1,582	928	300	346	83
1975-76	4,915	1,743	1,238	375	374	50
1976-77	6,598	2,420	(1)	(1)	473	59

* No disaggregated figures are available for this year.

(1) Primary and preparatory schools are being combined in the new Unity schools scheme thus abolishing this category.

Source: Democratic Yemen, Ministry of Education, reprinted in World Bank (1979).

Table 14: Teacher training

Year	No. of teacher training schools	No. of students		Female ratio
		Male	Female	
1966-67	3	150	90	60
1970-71	4	264	122	46
1973-74	4	278	130	47
1974-75	5	462	169	36
1975-76	6	563	231	41
1976-77	6	214	369	172

Source: Democratic Yemen, Ministry of Education and Maala Technical Institute, quoted in the World Bank Report (1978).

the breakdown of an earlier division of labour; but as teaching becomes progressively feminised it will be interesting to see whether it continues to hold the same attraction for men as it has in the past.

4. Industry and manufacturing

The manufacturing sector constitutes a significant employer of female labour, although it would appear that many women who are engaged in manufacturing are unpaid family labourers. Traditionally women worked in small family units producing items such as clothing and foodstuffs or engaged in packaging for the retail trade. While many of those engaged in these activities were originally Indian families in Aden, Yemeni women became increasingly involved as the port economy expanded.

The industrial sector in Democratic Yemen has experienced considerable growth in output, employment and number of enterprises since 1967, largely as a result of state support for import-substituting industries. Since 1968, 30–40 large industrial plants have been established and women have been encouraged to seek employment in these new enterprises in substantial numbers. A mixed pattern of ownership exists in industry, as elsewhere, with around 38 per cent of manufacturing in private hands, 28 per cent state owned, 24 per cent joint ventures, and 10 per cent owned by foreign interests. The larger enterprises such as the Aden refinery and the Sheikh Othman textile factory tend to be state owned, while the private sector accounts for a large number of small family enterprises, many of the artisan type. This latter sector none the less includes 13 factory-sized units producing clothing, shoes, paper products and food. The public and joint ownership sectors have experienced the most rapid growth and have approximately quadrupled their holdings since 1973 (World Bank, 1979).

The industrial sector generates work for some 17,000 men and women, roughly half of whom are employed in or around Aden. Thirteen thousand of this total are in the private sector, and the majority are likely to be in small enterprises. Although data are incomplete, we can assume that in small-scale manufacturing the percentage of unpaid family labour is high. Of the 5,000 or so workers in the larger enterprises, 1,800 are accounted for by the Aden Refinery and a further 1,234 by the textile factory at Sheikh Othman. The rest are distributed in units of 150 or fewer employees.

The more detailed information available on the female industrial workforce is confined to the 41 enterprises under the jurisdiction of the Ministry of Industry. These include units of various sizes ranging from four employees to 1,234, but most of them consist of medium size factories. Table 15 shows that out of a total workforce in this group of 3,675, women constituted 1,271 or 34.6 per cent.

Analysis of the structure of female employment in this sector conforms to the pattern found in other countries, namely that women are overwhelmingly represented in activities such as textiles and food processing. Within these enterprises, women tend to be concentrated in low or semi-skilled activities and few are promoted to, or trained for, managerial or supervisory positions. Even in the textile and clothes factories which typically exhibit a high concentration of female workers, the supervisors and managers tend, with few exceptions in the former case and none in the latter, to be men.

The same is true of the better-paid skilled jobs such as that of on-plant technicians. In every case known to me these were men. Although there are instances of women being trained to be mechanics, there were no women doing this job in any of the 14 factories I visited. The better-paid skilled labour in industry is largely the preserve of men.

This vertical division of labour by sex is complemented by a horizontal one which

44

Table 15: Figures for employment in factories and industrial establishments under the jurisdiction of the Ministry of Industry (December 1976)

Factories under the jurisdiction of the Ministry of Industry	Male	Female	Total employed
A. Public Sector Factories			
1. 'Revolution' spare parts factory	77	8	85
2. Agricultural and metallic implements factory	131	16	147
3. 'Soldier' plastics factory	33	16	49
4. Gas and oxygen factory	23	3	26
5. Spinning and textile factory	679	555	1,234
6. 'Martyrs' clothes factory	19	121	140
7. National tanning factory	65	10	75
8. Leather footwear factory	46	75	121
9. General establishment for soft drinks	244	34	278
10. General establishment for dairy products	31	7	38
11. General establishment for salt	281	5	286
12. Cereals mill	133	15	148
13. People's bakery	65	10	75
14. Tomato paste factory	74	36	110
Total (A)	1,901	911	2,812
(Women = 32.3% of employment in A)			
B. Mixed Sector Factories			
1. Aluminium factory	103	66	169
2. Perfume factory	13	23	36
3. Paint factory	36	4	40
4. Match factory	65	49	114
5. Yemeni rubber footwear factory	33	46	79
6. Sponge factory	29	3	32
7. Cigarette factory	76	77	153
Total (B)	355	268	623
(Women = 43% of those employed in B)			
Total (A) + (B)	2,256	1,179	3,435
(Women = 34.3% of A + B)			
C. Private Sector Factories			
1. 'Middle East' factory for plastic footwear	23	0	23
2. 'Aidrus' clothes factory	9	39	48
3. 'Fan Zin' national clothes factory	20	19	39
4. 'Saba' clothes factory	21	19	40
5. Woollen and semi-woollen clothing factory	13	7	20
6. Suitcase and belt factory	37	2	39
7. Nails factory	6	0	6
8. Ice factory	6	0	6
9. 'York' ice cream factory	6	0	6
10. 'Peninsula' paper bag factory	6	0	6
11. General Arab establishment for printing and paper bags	6	0	6
12. Mirror and glass factory	3	4	7
13. Detergents and insecticide factory	2	2	4
Total (C)	158	92	250
(Women = 36.8% of those employed in C)			
Total (A) + (B) + (C)	2,414	1,271	3,685
(Women = 34.4% of total employed in these three sectors)			

Source: Democratic Yemen, Ministry of Industry (1976, unpublished).

distributes women to certain jobs within the unskilled and semi-skilled categories, both at factory level and at the level of the labour process itself. At the factory level, women constitute the clerical staff, the sweepers and the cooks, while the discrete productive tasks are also divided up between the sexes. In the larger sewing factories, for example, only men will be found using the cutting machine and only the women will do button-holing. Such a division of labour is usually justified on the grounds that men are better equipped to handle larger machines whereas women are more capable of doing precision work.

We can conclude this chapter on employment with a few general observations. It is clear that on the one hand state policies have greatly assisted the entry of women into employment. The expansion of urban employment coupled with the encouragement given to women to seek paid work have combined with increased educational opportunities to break down traditional resistance against women working outside the home.

However, the kinds of jobs women both elect to do and are encouraged to do conform to a familiar pattern: women are to be found in the areas usually associated with least promotional possibilities, least pay and least status. Because wage differentials are not great in Democratic Yemen, this discrepancy is not as marked as in many other countries,[5] but wage differentials exist and their existence is significant. The implications of this will be explored in Chapter IV. As far as segregation in employment is concerned, this has not been broken down and there are cultural reasons why it might persist. In some cases, however, a *new* sexual division of labour has developed: in areas where men previously worked, women have now taken over and it appears that the status of the occupation has correspondingly fallen. Sewing and tailoring is a case in point. In Aden it was common in the pre-Independence period to find men and boys engaged in tailoring activities in small workshops, and this was regarded as a suitable occupation for men to do. Yet managers of clothing factories complained to me in 1977 that they were unable to attract a sufficient number of men to work in sewing factories, not only because the wages were lower than they might be able to earn elsewhere, but also because the influx of large numbers of women into sewing and textile factories had led to this work being identified with what were seen as "feminine" attributes. This, combined with the fact that large-scale factory work entails a loss of the traditional independence associated with the small workshop, led to fewer numbers of adult men seeking work in this area, although younger men and boys might enter it for a time, before moving on to more attractive employment.

NOTES

1) The basic data from which the following account is drawn is from the 1955 Census.
2) Figure given in the *Labour Force Bulletin* of Democratic Yemen, 1976 (Democratic Yemen, Central Statistical Organization, 1977). Women are included among those engaged in small shark drying and stripping workshops on the sea shore. The men beach and kill the sharks while the women butcher them and dry the pieces in the sun. Sharkmeat is a traditional source of protein for some of the people of the interior.
3) Men still outnumber women even in nursing. Institute of Health and Manpower Development figures for 1977–78 state that out of 79 trainee nurses only 11 were women. See table 12 for more detailed information.
4) Stenographers and personal assistants working for ministers and other senior officials were often men in 1977.
5) The monthly wage for unskilled industrial workers is 20 Yemeni Dinars per month compared with between 30 to 60 Yemeni Dinars for skilled and white collar employment (1978 figures).

CHAPTER IV

WOMEN FACTORY WORKERS

The influx of women into industrial employment and the formation of a sizeable female proletariat in the space of a generation is arguably one of the most striking achievements of the present government in Democratic Yemen. Yet it could be said that the reasons why women have entered industrial employment are relatively independent of government policies and merely reflect changes in the supply of, and demand for, female labour. It is of course true that on the demand side there has been an expansion in the employment opportunities for women accompanying both changes in official policy and the establishment of industries producing goods conventionally associated with female labour — textiles, clothing and food processing. It is probable that had this larger-scale industrial sector existed before Independence it might have attracted some women workers just as it is now doing.

Likewise, on the supply side, it can be argued that the economic imperatives for women to seek wage work, especially those from the poorest families, are strong. In addition, compared with some of the existing options for women, industrial employment has its attractions. It is stable, and unlike family labour, has fixed hours of work and is reasonably well paid.

Yet whatever truth there might be in this, the laws of supply and demand are not sufficient by themselves to account for the entry and departure of women from employment. The increase in female employment has been so rapid and so substantial, and compares so favourably with the record of other Muslim countries, that it is hard to deny the role of government policies in helping to bring about this situation. But just as it is possible to *underestimate* the role of government policies in bringing about profound transformations in the position of women it is also possible to *overestimate* the ease with which these transformations are accomplished.

In this chapter, which is divided into two parts, we will look in more detail at the position of women workers in order to analyse how the recent social and economic changes have affected their over-all position. In fact, what emerges from the research into the lives of female factory workers is that a great deal more than either the laws of supply and demand, or state policies so far, has been necessary to enable women to enter the labour force. Beyond the support given by the state to encourage women to enter full-time employment, and equally important, to remain in it, a number of ideological and material pre-conditions must also be met, some of which lie outside the realm of official intervention. The following section will focus on some of these pre-conditions and discuss the main influences which have operated at this level to facilitate the entry of these women into wage labour. In the second part we will consider the different factors which mitigate *against* women remaining in employment. By analysing those areas often hidden by official statistics it will be possible to discover the limits as well as the accomplishments of state policies. In the concluding section an assessment will be made of the twofold governmental aim of sexual equality and the mobilisation of women into the economically active population set against the reality of the position of female industrial workers.

1. A note on methodology

The data which are discussed in this section were gathered during a research visit to Democratic Yemen by the author in the latter half of 1977. They provide us with a rare insight into the character and composition of the female labour force in a developing socialist country. The opportunity to undertake interviewing of this kind in socialist countries is rarely extended to non-nationals and I am most grateful to those who made this work possible, as well as to the women who responded to my questioning. It was, ironically, not my original intention to work on the basis of a formal questionnaire. I had hoped instead to be able to conduct in-depth interviews with women workers in order to construct their life histories. This was not possible and instead a shortened version of my proposed questionnaire was officially approved as the basis of the research. This was supplemented with around 80 additional interviews with Party and State officials, factory and farm managers and a wide range of people from different walks of life.

The interviews discussed here were with women who worked in factories as semi-skilled or unskilled labourers. They were carried out at the respondents' place of work during working hours, which in Democratic Yemen are usually from 7 a.m. to 3 p.m. This had its positive and negative aspects. On the positive side, it enabled me to gain a considerable amount of lateral information about the conditions of work, the over-all sexual division of labour in industry and the attitudes of management to women workers, as well as to form a general picture of the female industrial workforce against which to check the profile that emerges from the interviews. On the negative side, the fact that the interviews were taking place during valuable production time meant that they had to be minimally disruptive and take up as little time as possible. Sometimes this meant interviewing individual women as they worked, sometimes it entailed interviewing them in groups. Occasionally a few questions had to be dropped because time was short that day.[1] On other occasions my informants were allowed to stay and chat to me after the interview was over and welcomed the chance to interview their interviewer about the position of women in the United Kingdom.

The women seemed to enjoy the group interview method the most. Invariably my questions would generate lively discussion and occasionally mirth, as with the enquiry as to whether men ever participated in the domestic chores. On the whole the atmosphere was relaxed and the responses friendly and forthcoming. This was probably helped by the fact that I insisted that no Party or factory official be present at the interview. The interviews were conducted in Arabic and with the assistance of an interpreter.

The sample was drawn from eight factories in Aden, which included small- and large-scale enterprises under different forms of ownership. Of these, two were state owned, two were private, one was a co-operative and three were mixed enterprises. The goods produced by these enterprises ranged from perfume to spare parts for agricultural machinery. The largest group of respondents (46.7 per cent) work in the Chinese-built textile factory at Sheikh Othman owned by the state; this is the second largest employer in Democratic Yemen with a total of 1,234 workers. It is also by far the largest single employer of female labour, and women account for over half of its total workforce. The respondents from this factory include both machine-minders, and workers involved in the dyeing and printing processes.

The second largest group (30 per cent) is comprised of women in sewing factories; they work predominantly as machinists but also as cutters and button-holers. These two groups, textile workers and seamstresses, spanning both state and private ownership, together comprise 70 per cent of the respondents. The rest of the sample is made up of small groups of machine-minders in the cigarette and match factory (6.7 per cent), packers in the perfume factory (5.8 per cent) and workers from the 14th October Press (5.8 per cent) and the spare parts factory (5 per cent). The occupational and factory distribution of these women can be seen from the tables below.

Table 16:   Respondent's employer

	No.	%
Spare parts factory	6	5.0
14th October Printing House	7	5.8
Sewing co-operative	7	5.8
Match and cigarette factory	8	6.7
S.O. Textiles	56	46.7
Perfume factory	7	5.8
El Aidrus sewing factory	7	5.8
'Martyrs' sewing factory	22	18.3
	120	100.0

Table 17:   Respondent's occupation

	No.	%
Seamstress	36	30.0
Machine operator (textile, match factory)	55	45.8
Binder	7	5.8
Packer	10	8.3
Welder/turner	6	5.0
Supervisor	6	5.0
	120	100.0

51

Although I have every reason to believe that the quality of the data is reasonably good, a few words need to be said in relation to the findings as a whole. The sample can be treated as fairly representative of women workers in recently established factories, although each factory had a different way of satisfying my request that it be randomly selected. Sometimes I was allowed to choose my own respondents, sometimes I interviewed all the women on a given production line, sometimes all the women in a given factory. On other occasions some respondents were selected for me. I have been able to detect no significant variations in the responses of women from different factories to suggest that any group is particularly skewed. However, some allowance must be made for the fact that in a small minority of cases some respondents would have been selected for interview by the administration because they were particularly good workers, or political activists or because they were considered among the better educated in the factory. There might also be a slight bias against older women on these grounds as they would be thought to be least likely to share the assumptions of the younger, more educated and politicised women.[2]

Unfortunately, the absence of the relevant census data against which this sample could be tested makes it impossible to assess the extent to which the sample is skewed with respect to characteristics such as educational level or marital status. Democratic Yemen is a poor country whose post-Independence government is only half way through its second decade and the official statistics which have so far been produced are few; some data are unreliable and some have been categorised in such a way as to obscure the information required. What we can say is that these industrial workers are clearly not representative of the female population taken as a whole, or of the female working population: the latter would include rural and unemployed women whose very different situation may be expected to find reflection in many of the crucial indicators. But the sample may be considered to be representative of female factory workers in the modern sector of industry, providing that allowance is made for a possible bias towards particular occupations. As rigorous adjustments and weightings cannot be made to account for any possible skewness, the data have been presented in the simplest way possible, enabling readers to make allowances where necessary.

1. Age, education and training

Perhaps the first point to be made about Democratic Yemen's female industrial workers is that in the 14 factories which I visited, the majority of women workers were in their teens or early twenties. Of the 120 women interviewed, 78 per cent were under 26 years old and nearly 40 per cent were between 18 and 20. This of course conforms to the picture of industrial women workers found in many other countries in the Third World, particularly where there has been an expansion in labour-intensive industry requiring unskilled or semi-skilled labour.

In the case of Democratic Yemen, this means that the majority of female industrial workers lived their early childhood in the pre-revolutionary period and their late childhood and teens in the decade of rapid change following Independence. In this sense they are a transitional generation caught between the old and the new societies. This finds reflection in their somewhat uneven educational level. Despite the restricted opportunities for female education in the pre-Independence period where in 1967 girls made up only 25 per cent of the school population, the level of educational attainment among the women interviewed was relatively high, especially given that most of these women were unskilled workers. Only 24 out of 120 (20 per cent) had received no formal education of any kind, but all except five of these 24 had received literacy classes and had passed their competence tests. Of those who had been to school (80 per cent), 21 had spent between four and five years in school and the same number had managed to complete six years of primary school. Thirty-five (29.2 per cent) had progressed to intermediate level and had spent between seven and nine years in school, and six women had studied for between 10 and 12 years.

Table 18: Educational level by respondent's age

Age	No. of years respondent spent in school								Only literate*		Total	
	Under 2		2–6		7–9		10⁺					
	No.	%	No.	%	No.	%	No.	%	No.	%	No.	%
16–18	1		10		10		–		–		21	
19–21	5		17		14		4		1		41	
22–25	9		6		6		2		8		31	
26–29	5		3		5		–		4		17	
30–45	1		6		–		–		3		10	
Total	21	17.5	42	35	35	29	6	5	16	13.3	120	100

* These respondents had no formal education but were literate, and had passed their literacy tests.

Source: Author's research.

This relatively high incidence of at least some educational attainment among the respondents is due to the fact that an education of some kind, or at the very least, literacy, is required of wage workers in the state sector of Democratic Yemen. In addition, the Aden Employment Bureau through which many of the industrial vacancies are filled, favours jobseekers with some education. In practice older workers might be able to trade experience for the education they missed, but younger urban workers seem to have benefited from both the expansion in education and from the factory-level literacy classes.

Given the recent expansion in educational opportunities for women, it is not surprising to find that the majority of respondents under 22 years of age had had several years of formal schooling while the women over 28 were the most educationally deprived. As can be seen from table 18, those who had received 10 or more years of schooling were all under 25 years of age, and all of the women who had received between seven and nine years of education were 28 and under. Conversely, most of the 10 women in the 30–45 year age group had had little formal education beyond the minimum. Some had attended primary school for a few years, and some had done so as mature students, but no women in this age group had had any kind of secondary education. Table 18 shows the age and educational distribution of the respondents.

The educational level of respondents shows some variation when cross-tabulated with both their occupation and their enterprise, although few of these findings are statistically significant. Moreover, the correlations suggested by the data must be weighed against such factors as management policies on recruitment, prevailing attitudes towards certain types of work, the length of time a factory has been in operation and whether an education is regarded as essential to the job in question. As indicated before, state-run enterprises tend to use education, or at least literacy, as a screening device for the selection of recruits, whereas private factories are less consistent in this regard. As table 19 shows, in the part privately owned cigarette and match factory, three out of the six women interviewed had received no education at all and were not even literate.

Table 19:   Respondent's occupation by number of
years spent in school

| | No. of years spent in school | | | | | |
	Under 2	2–6	7–9	10[+]	Only literate	Total
Sewing machinist	3	10	9	2	12	36
Textile factory worker – machine minder	5	17	11	1	–	34
Textile factory worker – fabric printer	1	8	5	–	–	14
Match factory – machine minder	6	1	–	–	–	7
Printing worker – binder or printer	1	–	6	–	–	7
Packer	1	2	3	–	4	10
Welder or turner	3	3	–	–	–	6
Supervisor	1	1	1	3	–	6
Total	21	42	35	6	16	120

Source: Author's research.

Similarly many of the 12 sewing machinists who had not gone to school were in private firms. Yet two of the four welders in the state-run spare parts factory were in the same position, appearing to contradict the general rule that state-run enterprises favour employees with some educational background. The explanation for this counter-instance probably lies in the fact that these women missed out on education as a result of having been brought up in the more educationally deprived rural areas. Moreover, although welding is a relatively skilled occupation, it is none the less regarded as a "dirty job" and not one suitable for women. The women recruited into these occupations are therefore likely to come from the poorer and more deprived sections of the population. It is worth noting that two of the group of six turners and welders in this factory had been channelled through the rural-based technical training centres, where they had acquired at least some formal education.

While these were the groups with the lowest educational level over-all, those with the highest were the supervisors, and the workers in the sewing and textile factories. Of the 70 respondents in this group, 50 had had between 2 and 12 years of formal education. Within this category more of the textile workers had completed primary *and* secondary school than the seamstresses, and the two textile factory supervisors had 10 or more years of schooling. This probably reflects the fact that recruitment to the textile factory was channelled through the government labour exchange. As a prestige project and state enterprise, the textile factory would be likely to both attract some of the better educated jobseekers, and receive them through the employment exchange.

2. Training

Most of the jobs women perform in industry are regarded as unskilled, whether they are or not, and there are few requirements beyond literacy and basic competence to discourage women from applying for work of this kind.[3] Unskilled workers are given in-plant training, and depending on the nature of the work, can take anything from a fortnight to two months to achieve peak production performance.

For semi-skilled workers such as sewing machinists, a few factories provide a form of low-paid apprenticeship for girls, while government-assisted projects have also concentrated on helping women acquire the basic skills. A substantial percentage of the sewing machinists in the sample had been trained under the aegis of the General Union of Yemeni Women, while others had been trained by the Union and now worked in Union co-operatives or enterprises.

In general, the kind of work opportunities available to women do not demand high levels of education or training; likewise, women's generally lower education level is reflected in their sectoral allocation. At the same time it is worth noting that of the 35 women who had received between seven and nine years of education, 28 of these (23 per cent) are perhaps not fulfilling their potential in the labour force, especially if they remain employed as unskilled or semi-skilled labour. Thus while education may have facilitated women's entry into employment, it has not always guaranteed the full utilisation of their potential.

3. Family background and structure

Given the degree of familial control exercised over women in Muslim societies, we must assume that the decision to work in industry is taken in consultation with the immediate kin or affinal group, except in the few cases where relations have been completely severed.

Family attitudes towards women entering wage work are shaped by a variety of factors including the degree and nature of religious observance, class and social position, and the family's location in either an urban or rural setting. Table 20 shows that 94 of the 120 informants (78.3 per cent) were born and brought up in the First Governorate, i.e. in the area in and around Aden. The number born abroad (16) outnumbers those who migrated from the interior (10), and includes 10 who were born in Indonesia or Ethiopia, countries where sizeable communities from the Yemens formed in the nineteenth century.

Table 20: Percentage distribution of respondent's place of birth

Place of birth	No.	%
First Governorate (Aden area)	94	78.3
Hinterland	10	8.3
Y.A.R.	6	5.0
Other	10	8.3
Total	120	100.0

Source: Author's research.

However, the pattern was very different in the case of their parents and reflects a high degree of family mobility in the 25 years before Independence. Almost half of the respondents' fathers (47 per cent) had been born outside the First Governorate, and significantly more of their mothers (62.3 per cent). The table below shows the differential distribution between the parents.

Table 21: Respondent's parent's place of birth

Birthplace	Father		Mother	
	No.	%	No.	%
First Governorate	49	43.0	43	37.7
Hinterland	32	28.1	21	18.4
Y.A.R.	30	26.3	36	31.6
Other	3	2.6	14	12.3
Total	114	100.0	114	100.0

Source: Author's research.

In both cases there is a high percentage of transnational migration. In the case of the migrant fathers roughly half were internal migrants and half were born abroad; in that of the migrant mothers fewer were born in what was formerly known as South Yemen and 44 per cent were born abroad, the majority in what was formerly known as North Yemen.[4] The effects of migration on attitudinal changes, employment and family patterns is a subject which has not been sufficiently researched in the context of Democratic Yemen; at this stage we can only speculate that, as with migrant families everywhere, there may have been a greater readiness on the part of these families to break with traditional attitudes and practices as part of the attempt to adapt to and survive in the urban economy.

If family origin and mobility may be factors in explaining the access of these women to industrial employment, the class and social position of their fathers and husbands would also exercise an important influence. We do not have information on the fathers' employment history, but at the time of the survey most of the respondents' fathers were involved in urban occupations. As can be seen from table 22 below, the majority of fathers are traders, craftsmen, skilled and unskilled workers.

Table 22: Father's employment by educational level
of respondent

Father's occupation	No. of years respondent spent at school						
	Under 2	2–6	7–9	10+	Liter- ate	Total	%
Medium to high level administrator, professional	–	–	2	–	–	2	1.6
Trader/merchant	3	4	6	2	3	18	15.0
Peasant, fisherman	4	2	1	–	1	8	6.6
Transport worker	1	5	3	–	1	10	8.3
Craftsman, skilled worker	4	7	2	3	3	19	15.9
Manual worker, unskilled	2	7	7	–	4	20	16.6
Security, armed	4	3	1	–	1	9	7.5
White collar	–	4	4	–	–	8	6.6
Other*	3	10	9	1	3	26	21.6
Total	21	42	35	6	16	120	100.0

* Includes 14 deceased or missing, and five retired or unemployed.

Source: Author's research.

This table also indicates that most of the better educated women came from families where the father was in one of the higher status occupations. The fathers of five of the six respondents with 10 or more years in school were either merchants, craftsmen or skilled workers, while among the eight daughters of peasants and fishermen, one had never been to school, and four had had under two years of schooling.

Moreover, as can be seen from table 23, the father's occupation also appears to correlate in some cases with that of their daughters. The bookbinders and printworkers come from families where the father is a white collar worker or a craftsman. The fathers of the supervisors were also white collar workers, small merchants or craftsmen, all occupations requiring a reasonable educational level. The packers, by contrast, have fathers who are or were peasants and labourers, a background shared by the workers in the match factory. These latter two categories, it will be remembered, were also those with the lowest educational level. Over half of the women seamstresses had fathers who were in trade, while, more significantly perhaps, a similar percentage of textile machine workers' fathers were manual labourers, many of them industrial workers.

The respondents' mothers were overwhelmingly housewives with no stated income-generating activity. This applied to both the past and present situations. The five exceptions were: two cooks, one school messenger, one peasant and one nurse. With the exception of the case where the mother was a peasant, all the respondents with wage-earning mothers were married women in their teens or early twenties. Since only 4 per cent of the women had working mothers, it therefore appears to have been extremely unusual for these workers to have come from families where the mothers had some kind of paid employment; it may also be that other respondents did not report their mothers' income-generating work or unpaid family labour, especially if it was only undertaken intermittently. This all clearly requires further investigation before any firm conclusions are reached.

Table 23: Intergenerational occupational mobility:
Respondent's occupation by father's occupation

Respondent's occupation	Father's occupation									
	Admin./ prof.	Trader	Peasant fisherman	Transport	Crafts- man, skilled	Manual labourer	Security	White collar	Other	Total
Sewing machinist	–	10	2	2	7	3	2	4	6	36
Textile machine operator	–	1	2	5	4	10	5	–	7	34
Fabric printer	–	1	–	–	3	2	1	1	6	14
Match/cigarette machine op.	–	1	3	2	–	–	1	–	–	7
Printer/binder	2	1	–	–	–	1	–	2	1	7
Packer	–	–	1	1	1	3	–	–	4	10
Welder/ turner	–	3	–	–	2	1	–	–	–	6
Super- visor	–	1	–	–	2	–	–	1	2	6
Total	2	18	8	10	19	20	9	8	26	120

Source: Author's research.

When women marry it is their husbands rather than their parents who will influence their entry into wage labour and the question arises as to whether the husband's class is a significant factor here. Although we have no information on the husband's background there is likely to be some overlap between the class origins of the natal family and that of the husband. Most marriages are likely to have been arranged by the parents or at least to take place with their approval; if they follow the traditional injunction to seek "equality of status", that is to marry within the same caste, tribe or descent status (known in the Hadramaut region as *Kafa'ah*), we would expect to find some similarity between the status and class of the two generations. What we do see is some indication of the effect of socio-economic change on the class structure of Democratic Yemen. The daughters of craftsmen, manual labourers, merchants and tradesmen are in turn marrying craftsmen and skilled workers, but they are also marrying white collar workers and lower level administrators. This seems to reflect a pattern which emerges in many transitional societies where certain occupations such as trade are regarded as desirable in the pre-capitalist urban economy, but are displaced in prestige terms by white collar jobs as the latter become more accessible with the advent of mass education, and more widely available with the expansion of the state sector.[5] A further indication of these changes is provided by table 24 on the husband's occupation which shows that, as with the fathers, the number of rural workers is negligible: whereas eight of the fathers were peasants or fishermen, only one of the workers' husbands was involved in agricultural work and he was employed in a recently established state-run chicken farm near Aden.

Table 24: Intergenerational mobility:
Father's occupation by husband's occupation

Father's occupation	Husband's occupation									
	Admin./ prof.	Trader	Peasant/ fisherman	Transport	Crafts-man, skilled	Manual labourer	Security	White collar	Other	Total
Admin./prof.	–	–	–	–	1	–	–	–	–	1
Trader	2	–	–	1	1	–	2	1	–	7
Peasant/ fisherman	–	–	–	–	1	1	–	1	1	4
Transport	1	–	–	1	2	–	1	–	–	5
Craftsman, skilled	4	1	–	–	1	1	2	–	–	9
Manual labourer	–	–	–	–	5	1	2	–	1	9
Security	–	–	–	1	1	1	–	2	–	5
White collar	–	–	1	–	–	–	–	1	–	2
Other	1	–	–	–	5	2	1	3	2	14
Total	8	1	1	3	17	6	8	8	4	56

Source: Author's research.

Over-all, then, almost half of the respondents are at least second generation Adenis and their immediate kin and affinal ties are largely urban-based. In contrast to the proletariat of some Third World cities, they are not migrant peasants and it is unlikely that their parents were either. They come, instead, from families with an involvement in the urban economy and skilled in urban occupations; their ties, cultural and economic, with the rural areas are consequently likely to be weak. Further research into the caste and class origin of these proletarian families, and into the degree to which the veiling and seclusion of women was practiced in the different areas from which they came, would cast valuable light on the question of how far attitudes have changed from one generation to another. This would make it possible to establish whether the family background of these workers is particularly conducive to their entry into the labour force; if this is not the case, then the attitudinal changes that have taken place in the space of a few generations are very striking indeed.

4. Marital status

How far marital status and fertility affect women's place in the labour market is subject to some cross-cultural variation, although it appears generally true that while marriage does not necessarily prevent women from entering wage work, the responsibility for children, particularly for the under-fives, often does.

Democratic Yemen follows the pattern of most Muslim countries where marriage is a near-universal phenomenon and only a very small percentage of women remain unmarried (see Youssef, 1973). Most urban women expect to be married or at least engaged by the time they reach their late teens. The age of marriage for rural women is far lower, 16 being the legal, but often violated minimum. Women generally marry at a younger age than men, and a three to five year gap is considered ideal. Our sample lends some support to the argument that women's entry into wage labour is associated in many cases with the postponement of marriage by a few years, since 25 of the 50 unmarried women interviewed were in their twenties, and the majority were between 20 and 25. The age of marriage among the older women was far lower than among the younger respondents, although one notable exception, a 17 year old who had been married (not just engaged) at the age of three months (sic) caused a stir when she mentioned this fact to her workmates.[6] If three months was the earliest, if atypical, age

Table 25: Marital status by age of respondent

Current age of respondent	Engaged women	Never married	Married women*					
			Age at marriage					
			Under 7	8–14	15–16	17–20	21–22	23+
16–18	1	13	1	–	4	2		
19–20	4	20	–	–	1	10		
21–22	–	6	–	–	–	4	2	
23–25	–	7	1	4	8	3	1	1
26–29	1	1	–	6	5	2	1	1
30–32	–	2	–	–	–	–	–	–
33–37	–	–	–	2	1	3	1	–
38–45	–	1	–	–	–	–	–	–
Total	6	50	2	12	19	24	5	2

* Includes widows and divorcees (total 64).

Source: Author's research.

of marriage in the sample, 28 years was the highest, giving a mean of 17 years for all married women including divorcees and widows.[7] Of all married respondents 64 per cent had been married at between 15 and 20 years of age. As can be seen from the preceding table only four women married between the ages of 23 and 28, whereas 25 married at the age of 14 or under. The older women were in almost every case those who had experienced an early first marriage and some of these were now divorcees.

5. Married workers

In many Third World countries unmarried women are more likely to be working than are married women,[8] but given the universality of marriage in Muslim countries and the low age of marriage for women, we would expect to find a significant percentage of married women in the labour force. In our sample, 64 women had married out of which 45 were still living with their husbands. The remaining 19 were widows and divorcees. Of the 45 still married almost half were 22 years old and under, and over 90 per cent were under 30 years old. It is interesting to note that 18 of the 45 women in active conjugal relationships had been in their present job for under two years, 20 for between three and four years and the remaining seven for between five and seven years. Fourteen respondents had had some previous employment experience, usually for under two years. Eight of these were married at the time they entered employment. Over-all, there appears to be no significant difference between the single and married women with respect to work experience and duration of employment. There are certainly fewer married women living with husbands in the sample than single, divorced and widowed together, but at 37.7 per cent they represent a fairly high proportion none the less. Not surprisingly, the attitude of the majority of husbands to their wives taking up paid employment was reported to be positive. But 5 out of 45 (10.4 per cent) were said to have viewed the situation negatively. Two women said their struggle with their husbands over whether they should work or not almost led to divorce. It is worth noting that despite the importance of the husband's approval in helping to shape the women's attitude to their work, over half (54.4 per cent) of the married women had entered employment before getting married. The majority, then, had their parents as their primary reference point and are most likely to have entered employment with their approval.

Most of the women did not see marriage as an alternative to wage work. Of the single women 69.1 per cent said they would continue to work after they married, 21.8 per cent said they would leave and 9.1 per cent were not sure. Of this last group some volunteered that they would defer to their future husband's wishes, while others said that their decision would depend simply upon whether they could afford to give up their earnings or not. The majority of those who thought that they would continue working after marriage were in their teens or early twenties, whereas those who were noncommital or opposed to combining wage work and marriage were spread fairly evenly through the sample. The greatest degree of diffidence vis-à-vis working after marriage was exhibited among the seamstresses, only 35.7 per cent of whom said they would work after marriage; a majority (42.9 per cent) said they would leave work if they married and 21.4 per cent said they were not sure. It is possible that leaving work in this case meant leaving the *place* of work. Seamstresses can expect to be able to carry on some work at home and it appears that many of them do.

61

Thus it would seem that for the respondents in this sample marriage in itself is not seen as an insurmountable obstacle to women remaining employed and that husbands' attitudes are, on the whole, positive. Yet it is reasonable to assume that many women do leave paid employment when they marry or are prevented from taking it up by their husbands. Thus the relatively high rate of husband approval in the sample could be seen as an unusual and very important pre-condition for women remaining in paid work.

6. Household structure

The size and composition of the households of women workers can be important in determining the kinds of domestic pressures they are subjected to, as well as providing useful demographic information regarding the possible effects on fertility of women entering wage work.

While detailed evidence on household structure and composition in Democratic Yemen is not yet available, the survey reveals a fairly high incidence of the nuclear family form in both the respondents' childhood homes and in their present households. Only 32.5 per cent (39) of the respondents grew up in extended families while 67.5 per cent (81) grew up in nuclear families. How typical this pattern is of this generation of Adeni families cannot of course be assessed in the absence of the appropriate statistics for comparison; but the high incidence of the nuclear form in the childhood homes of those interviewed may bear some relation to the high level of migration among the parents of the respondents.

As far as the present domestic arrangements are concerned, table 26 shows the preponderance of the nuclear family form with 69 per cent (83) of the respondents living in nuclear families — a similar percentage of women having been brought up in nuclear families as now living in them. Among the women interviewed the setting up of nuclear households was certainly seen as a desirable goal and one which was thought to be attainable, if resources permitted, at the time of marriage.

Table 26: Family type by marital status

Family type	Married	Divorced	Widowed	Single	Engaged	Total
1. Ego lives in extended family which includes husband (if alive, and not divorced), children, and parents	8	3	2	–	–	13
2. Ego lives in conjugal, nuclear family	22	–	–	–	–	22
3. Ego lives with neither husband nor parents, but alone or with relatives	3	3	1	8	1	16
4. Ego lives in parental nuclear family home	9	7	2	38	5	61
5. Ego lives in parental extended family	3	1	–	4	–	8
Total	45	14	5	50	6	120

Source: Author's research.

Table 26 not only shows the considerable variations in household composition, but also how these are related to the marital status of the respondents. For example, 83.9 per cent (47) of the 56 single women lived with their parents, as is customary in most Muslim countries. Once married, couples generally try to set up their own (conjugal) households. We can see that half of the married women in the sample had succeeded in doing this, while the rest remained in the parents' household, or, as is more common in Democratic Yemen, moved in with their husband's family. This latter course is nearly always thought to be unsatisfactory as a long-term solution and the usual reason given is the tension it generates between mothers and daughters-in-law. Traditionally, new brides brought into the patrilocal family were made to work for the mother-in-law and, according to popular accounts, they frequently suffered ill treatment at the mother-in-law's hands. Nowadays, however, where young brides may be wage-earners, the mother-in-law may well lose her traditional hold over her son's wives; as we shall see later the evidence suggests that she may even be converted into her daugther-in-law's domestic helpmate. Despite this assistance women workers may receive from the mothers-in-law they still seem to prefer to establish their own households, even if the cost may be that a greater burden of domestic labour is borne by themselves.

Most women therefore seem anxious to escape the confines of their natal and affinal families, and see marriage as the chief means of doing this. None the less it is to the natal family that they can return for refuge in the event of divorce, desertion or widowhood. Table 26 shows that 11 of the 14 divorcees and four of the five widows lived with parents and these would in every case be their own parents and not their affines. The difference, however, is that, in the past, such women would be the financial responsibility of their kin. Although divorced women might have a portion of their bride price returned to them, they would not be expected or allowed to become self-supporting for fear of dishonouring the family name. Yet the fact that 15.8 per cent (19) of the workers interviewed were divorced or widowed is testimony to the change in attitudes that has occurred. At the same time the change in women's material circumstances with increased employment opportunities has reduced their economic dependency on both marriage and on their families. Some women explained that in the past they had been afraid to seek divorce because their parents could not afford to support them, but now with wage work available to them, they have acquired a greater margin of choice. The reportedly high rate of divorce in Democratic Yemen is attributed by government officials primarily to this factor.

7. Household size

Democratic Yemen has traditionally been a society in which children are highly valued, and the tendency has been until now to encourage large families. The mean family size in Democratic Yemen is 5.4, and is somewhat higher, at over 6, in the rural areas. The total fertility rate is estimated to be 6.1 for the country as a whole (see UN ECWA, 1980). It is well established that high fertility coupled with an early age of marriage and childbearing produce a situation which is antithetical to women's entry into the labour force. However, in the case of the industrial workers in the sample two findings are especially interesting: first, among these workers there was a striking degree of agreement as to their preference for a smaller than average family size;

63

second, the age of childbearing is later than the apparent norm, just as the age of marriage is considerably later than for rural women and some categories of urban women. Thus for these women workers the postponement of childbearing and marriage, and their preference for smaller families, may represent an attitudinal shift of a significant kind.

As far as the size of the respondents' households is concerned, the survey reveals that the mean household size is 5.9, somewhat higher than the 1973 census figure for Aden (5.4). Table 27 shows that the smallest household in the sample was comprised of two and the largest consisted of 18 members, with the majority of households (66.4 per cent) falling into the smaller, 2–6 member category.

Table 27: Number of persons in respondent's household

No. of persons in household	No. of respondents	%
1–2	10	8.8
3–4	31	27.4
5–6	34	30.1
7–10	27	23.9
11–18	11	9.7
	113	100.0

Source: Author's research.

These findings are interesting but they do need qualifying. The households represent different stages in the life cycle; some of them are the respondent's natal families, and some are conjugal. It must also be borne in mind that given the relatively young age of most of the women in the sample their families will in many cases be incomplete and this may give a misleading impression of a relatively small household size.

We can turn to another variable to cast light on this question, namely the respondents' views on family size. Given the positive values attached to large families by the majority of people of Democratic Yemen, and given the government's concern to maintain a high birth rate, the answer to this question will be important in evaluating how far the attitudes of industrial workers have departed from these more conventional views.[9] When the respondents were asked what they thought the ideal number of children to have was, almost half (47.5 per cent) replied that two children was ideal and comparatively few favoured large families. It should, however, be stressed that there is often a considerable disjuncture between expressed preference and behaviour in this area. Although women may want fewer children, they frequently end up having more than they would ideally like, and this occurs for a variety of reasons ranging from kin or marital pressure to bear sons, to the lack of birth control measures.[10] The fact that women workers appear to want fewer children is none the less significant, especially as it is at variance with government policy in this question.

As can be seen from table 28, attitudes on this question showed some variation according to the age of the respondent. With the exception of one 20 year old who

Table 28: Respondent's preference for number of children desired by age (in %)

Respondent's age	Ideal number of children										Mean
	0	1	2	3	4	5	6	7	10	14	
16–18		1	14	1	2	2	1				2.6
19–20		2	21	4	5	2			1		2.7
21–22			3	3	6						3.2
23–25	1	1	11	4	6	1	1				2.8
26–29		1	5	4	4		1	1		1	3.8
30–36		1			2	1		1			4.2
37–45		1	3		1						2.2
Total	1 (0.8)	7 (5.8)	57 (47.5)	16 (13.3)	26 (21.6)	6 (5)	3 (2.5)	2 (1.6)	1 (0.8)	1 (0.8)	

Source: Author's research.

thought 10 was the ideal number of children to have, the majority of respondents under 25 years favoured a maximum of two children. Those who favoured larger families (five children and over) tended to be in their late twenties and thirties, although some of the women who thought one child sufficient were also in this age group. This seems to indicate a fairly recent change of attitude.

A substantial number of women volunteered that ideally they would want an equal number of girls and boys, a view which is again in marked contrast to traditional preferences which were strongly biased against girl children, since it was sons who increased the power of the family and the lineage.[11] The difference in attitudes towards family size between traditional and modern, rural and urban, is particularly evident here, and reflects a significant departure from the conventional views. Unfortunately it was impossible to obtain any information about the husbands' preferences, but it is likely that even among men, previous attitudes have gradually been eroded by the experience of urban life, and by the practicalities of urban living conditions. The shortage of housing space, for example, must affect views on family size; at the same time, the traditional reasons, material and ideological, for wanting large families that prevail in rural society no longer apply under the changed circumstances of urban living.

If industrial workers seem to want fewer children they also have their children later than is usual in many Middle Eastern countries; this is a factor of major importance since it is precisely the postponement of child-rearing which makes possible the entry of many women into the labour force. In the sample, only four women out of 24 who were under 23 years of age had had children. This finding is in marked contrast to figures given in a MCH report which puts the average child-bearing age of 1,000 women who attended clinics in Aden in 1976 at 18. Significantly, most of these women were housewives and none were industrial workers.

It is interesting to note that of the 45 ever-married women 38 per cent were childless. Of these, 13.3 per cent had been married for under a year, 13.3 per cent for one year, 6.6 per cent for two years, 2.2 per cent for three years, and 2.2 per cent for four years. Thus, 24.3 per cent of these childless women had been married for a year or more. This postponement of childbearing suggests that family planning was accepted by at least some women as a necessary concomitant of wage work.

On the other hand, the number of married women with children (25) was greater than those without (20), and over-all constituted a fairly high percentage of the total sample at 22.5 per cent. The percentage rises to 33.3 per cent if divorcees and widows are included. The number of children the respondents had varied from one to eight with a mean of 2.8. Predictably, this showed considerable variation according to the respondents' ages. Given the relatively few older women represented in the sample, it is not surprising to find that the largest number of women with children was in the 23–28 year age group; this accounted for three-quarters of all those with children. Within this group the number of children varied considerably; five of the women had one child, nine had two, nine had three or four children, one had five and two women aged 28 had more than seven children. Table 29 below shows the over-all distribution of children among the married women respondents.

Table 29: Distribution of number of
children for married women

No. of children	No. of married women*
None	20
1	7
2	4
3–4	9
5–6	2
7–8	3
Total	45

* Excludes divorcees and widows.

Source: Author's research.

Although the number of children they have is an important variable for younger mothers, since it is likely that their children will be young and need greater care and attention, the same does not necessarily apply to older women. For these women the day-to-day responsibilities would be somewhat less, since their children would be old enough to take care of themselves. The number of children, though greater for older women, does not by itself constitute an obstacle to working for women at this stage in their life cycle; in some circumstances it may even constitute an advantage, since the older children may assume some responsibility for younger siblings.

Table 30: Age of married women and number of children
(excludes divorcees and widows)

Age	No. of women	No. of women with children	Mean no. of children
17–18	5	2	1.0
19–20	11	1	1.0
21–22	6	1	1.0
23–25	9	8	2.3
26–29	10	9	3.95
30–37	4	4	3.75
Total	45	25	

Source: Author's research.

8.   Housework and child-care

In most societies the participation of women in the labour force is restricted by the fact that they retain primary responsibility for domestic work and child-care. The responsibilities of housework and child-care combined with employment impose a heavy burden on women and restrict their capacity for taking a place in the labour force as the equals of men.[12]

In Democratic Yemen no official support has yet been given to *equalising* male/female domestic roles; as a result domestic labour and child-care are still almost entirely carried out by women. Men continue to regard this work as demeaning and appear to do the minimum prescribed by custom and necessity. Of the 115 respondents with men in their households, 68.6 per cent claimed to receive no help at all from them; those who did receive help (30.4 per cent) said that it came mostly from small boys, sons or younger brothers (51 per cent or 18 cases), and from husbands (40 per cent or 14 cases). Of those women who had help from men 80 per cent were either married or divorced and the nature of the assistance they were given appears to correlate with the kind of household they were living in. The cases of husbands helping out were all from small families, the majority conjugal units with a mean family size of 3.9. By contrast, husbands were relieved from the pressure to do this work in the larger families by the presence of other female kin and of small boys who could perform some of the household tasks. The 18 cases where respondents received help from

67

small boys were in these larger households with a mean family size of 7.3. In no case were older men (fathers, grandfathers, uncles, etc.) said to contribute to domestic tasks, and in no case where a married couple had a father in residence did the husband assist his wife in household tasks. It is interesting in this respect that of the 35 cases where men or boys helped out, the majority of them (24) had no fathers in residence. It is not unreasonable to suppose that fathers might resist any erosion in their households of the sexual division of labour upon which male authority traditionally rested. A number of respondents complained that their fathers' attitudes were "old-fashioned" and that it was wrong of them to continue to expect their daughters to perform personal service on their behalf. Several women complained that when they returned from work they had to wait on their retired or unemployed fathers "hand and foot". As one women explained: "I spend 11 hours out of the house, travelling to work and working, and when I get home in the evening my father who has been at home all day expects me to wait on him like a servant. He snaps his fingers and calls for water, and if I complain he accuses me of losing my respect for my elders."

It is precisely this kind of problem that many women hope will be overcome through setting up a new home on marriage. Certainly women's husbands appeared to be less demanding than their fathers although there was a clear understanding that the wives' main area of responsibility was the home and children. Of the 45 married women in the sample about half claimed to receive some household help from their husbands, and as we saw above, this was especially the case where the couple lived on their own. But the only women who claimed that their husbands did as much domestic work as they did were two Party members, neither of whom had children. Even if these husbands only contributed a fraction of the work of their wives, the response indicates an encouraging awareness among some Party members of the importance of the issue. In general the fact that some husbands help out at all indicates an important generational change since it is doubtful whether these men's fathers would have thought it proper to assist in household tasks at all.

Leaving aside these two exceptions, however, the contribution made by men to domestic work tended to be restricted to what women described as "light tasks", helping occasionally with the cooking and more substantially the shopping. In countries with a legacy of *purdah* restrictions young men or servants would normally do the shopping, and it seems that this continues even when the women of the household are no longer in strict seclusion. However, this pattern is breaking down with women's greater freedom of movement. With the difficulties of shopping in a country that experiences substantial shortages, men may be less prepared to continue to perform this role for the sake of tradition alone. As far as cooking was concerned, while a few husbands were prepared to help out, this tended not to be a regular commitment so much as an occasional "favour" if the wives were ill or visiting parents. This was also true of the other activities men performed in the home.

The picture with regard to child-care is even more one-sided. In no case were men said to assume any major responsibility for child-care and there was said to be almost no "helping out"; child-care was regarded as being quintessentially "women's work" by women as well as men. So, given that in 70 per cent of cases women received no help from the men in their households for housework, and in every case women had exclusive responsibility for child-care, women workers in Democratic Yemen would appear to be caught in the classic problem of the "double shift".

Yet this is not quite the case because of an important countervailing factor.

Many of the women workers interviewed were to some extent released from their burden of domestic responsibilities by transferring it to their female relatives. As can be seen from table 31 below only 13 per cent of women had *sole* responsibility for

Table 31: Person who does the housework in respondent's home

	No.	%
Self alone	16	13
Self with others	26	22
Mother, mother-in-law	59	49
Other female kin	19	16
Total	120	100

Source: Authors' research.

housework in their households, while 65 per cent relegated *primary* responsibility to female kin. The remainder, 22 per cent, shared the housework with other relatives. Of the respondents, 49 per cent — typically younger women still living at home — said that their mothers did the housework, and in 64 per cent of all cases mothers (or mothers-in-law) made some contribution to the housework, often with other female members of the household. In other words *only 35 per cent of the women workers in this sample performed some or all of the household duties themselves and only 13 per cent had sole responsibility.* The pattern varies significantly for married and single women. Of the 56 single (never married) women only 8.3 per cent (10) did any housework themselves. Of the remainder, 57.1 per cent (32) had help from their mothers, and 25 per cent (14) had help from female kin other than their mothers. By contrast, nearly seven times the number of married women did their own housework; of the 45 married women, 57.7 per cent (26) did the household chores themselves, while mothers assumed most of the burden in only 35.5 per cent (16) of the cases and in only 6.6 per cent (3) of the cases was it assumed by other female kin.

The same pattern of reliance on female support can be discerned in the case of child-care, with one significant difference. Whereas married women tend to receive less help for *housework* from female kin than their unmarried counterparts, they do receive help for *child-care*. Indeed, 80 per cent of the 40 working mothers (including widows and divorcees) relied on female kin to care for their children while at work, and in most cases this help came from the children's grandmothers. In 41.9 per cent of the cases, grandmothers had exclusive responsibility for child-care and in a further 53.5 per cent of the cases, the grandmothers played an auxiliary role, sometimes sharing the responsibility with the respondent's sisters or aunts. A few mothers, about 20 per cent, left their children alone during the day if they were old enough to fend for themselves. Two women left their smaller children in the care of an older daughter and in only one case was a child placed in one of the state-run kindergartens. It is important to emphasise that in no case did husbands assume any responsibility for child-care although a few occasionally "helped out". This usually meant taking their older children out for walks or watching over them at home while their mothers cooked or cleaned. Women pointed out that this in itself was a very recent development. It was confined to younger men with, as they put it, "more progressive attitudes". But even these men would never wish to be seen publicly in sole charge of infants.

We noted above how the position of working women vis-à-vis domestic labour tended to vary according to marital status. But there are other variables that must be taken into account, namely household size, structure and composition. As can be seen from the table below, household size has some bearing on the allocation of domestic tasks, in that the larger the household, the more likely the working women is to have other female kin available to help with the chores.

Table 32: Respondent's child-care arrangements and how they are affected by presence of other household members*

No. in present home	Self or left alone		Mother and other female kin		Other		Total	
		%		%		%		%
2–6	6	24	18	72	1	4	25	65.7
7–10	0	–	9	100	0	–	9	23.6
11–18	0	–	4	100	0	–	4	10.5
Total	6	15.7	31	81.5	1	2.6	38	100.0

* Married, divorced and widowed women with children only.

Source: Author's research.

In the case of child-care we saw that only 15.7 per cent of mothers had the sole responsibility of caring for their children, and these were all in conjugal nuclear families. By contrast, all of the mothers living in larger families had their children cared for them by female relatives. Table 32 shows that 76 per cent of those in the smaller households could still rely on their female relatives for some help. Sometimes this was because they shared a housing unit; but, even when they did not, mothers or sisters were still willing to assume this role, especially if they lived nearby. In most cases, an element of reciprocity was involved; money or services were exchanged; child-care was provided in exchange for the right to watch television, or for clothes being washed, or for a portion of the working mothers' wage.

Still, women with children are those under the most pressure from domestic responsibilities, despite the fact that working women in general are able to rely to a considerable extent on the services of their female kin, especially their mothers or mothers-in-law. The following table shows the respondents' own evaluation of their situation. Their responses to the question of whether they experienced any special difficulties as working women (and if so what were these) is correlated with marital status to reveal which women feel themselves to be under the most pressure, and why.

Table 33: Respondent's marital status and the difficulties experienced as a women worker

	Child-care		Role conflict		No time for edu- cation		No diffi- culties		Total
		%		%		%		%	
Married	13	29.5	4	9.1	1	2.2	26	59.1	44
Divorced	3	23.1	–	–	–	–	10	76.9	13
Widowed	–	–	–	–	–	–	5	100.0	5
Single/ engaged*	5	10.9	–	–	–	–	41	89.1	46
Total	21	19.4	4	3.7	1	0.9	82	75.9	100

* These women were referring to younger children.

Source: Author's research.

It is clear that 76 per cent (82) of the respondents claimed to experience no significant difficulties, and we must assume that this is related to the fact that they receive substantial help from their female relatives as far as housework and child-care are concerned. But of those who did experience difficulties, it is the married and divorced women who have the greatest difficulty and it is child-care which is cited as the greatest problem. The situation of this group is particularly important to understand. For, if Democratic Yemen is to rely on a stable female industrial labour force, it will have to confront the fact that most women are likely to marry and have children. If the problems of these women can be solved, it can draw on a larger number of potential workers and so reduce the turnover of those already in the labour force. Whereas only 10.9 per cent of single women experienced difficulties, the figure rises to 33.8 per cent of ever-married women. If we analyse in detail the situation of these 45 ever-married women, dividing them into those who did not experience difficulties and those who did, the reasons underlying their differential responses become clear. Taking those who experience *no* difficulties first, we find that 21 out of 24 (87.5 per cent) enjoyed one or more of what we can describe as key facilitating factors — no

71

children, large households (i.e. over six members) and mothers or mothers-in-law in residence. Of these 21 women, 16, i.e. 76 per cent, had no children, nine lived in families with seven or more members, and 11 had mothers or other female kin living in the family. If we compare this with the situation of those who did experience difficulties, we find that in 10 cases out of 21 there were children in the household, in 11 the families were small, often in the 2–4 member category, and in 14 cases there were no female relatives to help out. It is also significant that only six childless respondents in the whole sample complained of difficulties. In addition, only four who had mothers in the household and only three who lived in large households complained of difficulties.

Of the matrix of different factors which bear especially heavily on women workers it appears therefore that child-care is the most problematic, although it can be alleviated through support from female kin. The latter tends to be associated with living in larger families. Of the women who mentioned child-care as a special problem 80 per cent were in households with six or less inhabitants. And all of the women who mentioned the difficulty of reconciling the roles of mother and worker were also in this category of household size.

The data on housework and child-care suggest that in the larger families, the entry of some of the female members into industrial employment does not disturb the traditional sexual division of labour; rather it is more likely to produce a reordering of the female hierarchy. As younger female members of the family become wage-earners their mothers and other female kin take over their share of the domestic labour. In the conjugal households, however, and especially those where there are children, husbands come under greater pressure to help their wives; the effect of this is to produce a minor modification in the traditional division of labour between the sexes. Over-all, however, the burden of domestic responsibilities still falls disproportionately on the woman; even if the young woman worker escapes these while she lives with her parents or parents-in-law, she is unlikely to do so when she sets up her own home.

2. Attitudinal changes

It is obvious that relative to the population as a whole the urban working class in Democratic Yemen has undergone major attitudinal changes over the past 25 years, and although some of these have been accelerated to a considerable extent by government policies in the past decade others have occurred despite these policies. We have seen, in the earlier sections, that compared with previous attitudes and compared with some which are still prevalent, significant changes have taken place with regard to views on marriage and fertility, domestic relations and attitudes to work. To summarize the main findings, female industrial workers appear to:
1. prefer smaller families, the majority mentioning two children as the ideal number to have;
2. often postpone marriage until their early twenties;
3. often postpone childbearing to their early or mid-twenties;
4. generally do not see marriage as precluding wage work and express the desire to continue working after marriage; and
5. sometimes obtain some domestic help from their husbands.

In addition to these quite significant findings, we have further indicators which suggest both the direction of change and the attitudes of the women towards the effects of these changes on their specific situation. These indicators are: political involvement, the wearing of the *sheidor* and veil, and attitudes towards the main changes in the position of women since 1967.

Political activity is an area which is in many ways the most difficult for women to penetrate in any society, and this is especially the case in countries where the exclusion of women from public life was previously widespread. The general findings reported in Part I of this study are reflected in the data on political participation generated by the interviews. Among the informants, a fairly high percentage, 48.3 per cent (58 out of 120), were, or had been members of one or more of the mass organisations. Of these 36.7 per cent (44) were or had been in the General Union of Yemeni Women, and, of these, over a third were or had been active in at least one other political organisation, most commonly the Youth Organisation, of which a total of 30 women (25 per cent) over-all had been or were members. Only four (3.3 per cent) however, were or had been Party members, and only five (4.1 per cent) were active in the workers' commissions in the factories. However, 48 per cent of the sample with some kind of political involvement is a fairly substantial figure and may reflect the fact that women are encouraged to seek employment through political mobilisation. Most of these women with some political experience were under 30 years of age and of those who were or had been in the Women's Union, 43 per cent were under 22 years of age. It is interesting to note that being a member of the women's organisation did not appear to affect women's domestic situation. Only a quarter of the women in the Union received any help from men in the home, a slightly lower proportion than in the sample as a whole. Similarly, there were no significant differences in the attitude of members and non-members towards the wearing of the veil or sheidor. This would seem to reflect the relatively low priority accorded to such issues by the Women's Union.

1. Main changes since 1967

When we consider that these women workers have had to break with some of the traditional values and customs with which they grew up, the question may be posed as to how they view the changes that have occurred in Democratic Yemen since 1967. Most of the 113 who responded to this question singled out the changes in the position of women for special comment, although since the interviews had focused to a considerable extent on the position of women this is to be expected. More striking is what aspect of this was singled out for special mention: the largest group (38) noted, often with considerable enthusiasm, that women were no longer forced into seclusion since restrictions on their activities had eased and substantial desegregation had occurred. Seventeen women in this group thought that the granting of equal rights between the sexes was the major factor enabling this change to take place. As can be seen from table 34, women's entry into paid labour and education were also seen by a substantial percentage as the most significant changes seen since Independence, while for 12 women social and economic life in general had undergone such a complete transformation that as they expressed it, "all aspects of women's lives had been transformed". In general, judging from the warmth of the response (only eight women

73

refused to comment or reported no changes) it would seem that on the whole they viewed the direction of change positively.[13]

Table 34: Main changes since Independence as perceived by respondents

	No.	%
1. Women less secluded, greater sexual equality	38	33.6
2. The country has industrialised, greater number of factories	7	6.2
3. Nothing to say, no change	8	7.1
4. Women have entered employment	25	22.1
5. Women and girls being educated now	17	15.0
6. Everything has changed and women's position is transformed	18	15.9
Total	113	100.0

Source: Author's research.

2. Veiling

Compared with the Yemen Arab Republic and with many other countries in the Muslim world where the veiling of women remains widespread or is actually on the increase, the situation in Democratic Yemen appears to bear out the optimism of the Women's Union that these practices will diminish, at least in the urban areas, with changes in the wider economy and society.[14] On the streets of Aden, comparatively few women are completely veiled. Most wear only the *sheidor* and relatively few wear face veils. There are considerable variations in the way the *sheidor* is worn. Some women hold it tightly around their faces so that it functions as a half veil; others merely use it as a cloak draped loosely around their shoulders. According to a survey carried out by the author in the streets of Tawahi, the modern shopping and tourist centre of Aden, about 18 per cent of the women in the streets wear modern dress, or trousers, or knee-length skirts with blouses which cover the arms. However, the percentage is much lower in the more traditional urban settlements in Aden such as Sheikh Othman, and in the towns and villages outside Aden, Western dress is almost never worn. In Aden some women are making the transition to modern dress by wearing an overcoat, called by the Russian term *balto*, sometimes worn with a thin veil covering the face and hair.

Women's attitudes towards veiling were ambivalent, and can be summed up by the statement of one of the women workers who said, "I don't mind wearing the *sheidor*. If I don't wear it people will speak badly of me and say 'look she has no religion and no modesty'." Many women made a distinction between wearing the *sheidor*, which they did not see as particularly oppressive, and the face veil which they did. More than half of the women workers who wore the face veil complained that it was their families or husbands who enforced it, and that they themselves would prefer to do without it, although they were quite happy to wear the *sheidor*.

Women who work in factories in Democratic Yemen do not as a rule wear either *sheidors* or veils. Most wear shirts and trousers, sometimes supplied by the enterprise; some wear scarves which partially or completely cover their hair. This style of dress is worn even in factories which employ a large number of male workers. Yet despite the fact that women are generally unveiled at the workplace, only 24 per cent of the respondents wore neither sheidor nor veil on the street. On the other hand only 25 per cent wore *both* the sheidor and the veil on the street, so that over half the women were unveiled but wore their *sheidor,* sometimes only as a loose cloak. A few women had adopted the *balto* instead of the *sheidor* but this was often accompanied by the wearing of the veil. The age of the respondents did not necessarily determine what style of dress was adopted. The pattern among the younger women for instance shows considerable variation. Although 72 per cent of the women who wore neither *sheidor* nor veil were under 23 years of age, nearly half of the women who wore both *sheidor* and veil were in this age group too. Most women over 23 wore the *sheidor*, but not all of the women who wore neither *sheidor* or veil were younger women. Although the older women may cling more tenaciously to traditional practices, if they choose not to they are subject to fewer sanctions than the younger women. Unmarried women in particular are under pressure from their families to conform to the conventional standards of propriety and adopt modest dress. The types of occupations these women were involved in appeared to make little difference to their sartorial choice, although the seamstresses had the highest percentage of *sheidor* wearers of

Table 35:   Incidence and degree of veiling
among female factory workers

Veiling	Absolute number	%
Sheidor only	46	46.4
Sheidor and veil	25	25.2
Neither, no *hejab*	20	20.2
Scarf	1	1.0
Coat and veil	6	6.0
Coat	1	1.0
Total	99*	100.0

* Data for remaining cases unavailable.

Source: Author's research.

75

any group. The group of welders and turners for example, although conscious of being pioneers in doing work conventionally done by men, were distributed evenly among those who wore the *sheidor* and veil and those who wore neither, or at most a scarf.[15] A smaller proportion of women whose fathers were born in the First Governorate (Aden) wore the veil compared with those whose fathers were born in the hinterland. The daughters of white collar workers, administrators and transport workers all had a tendency to wear neither *sheidor* nor veil.

3.   The limiting factors

In the preceding sections we have considered some of the factors influencing and enabling women's participation in the urban labour force. These include not only government policies but a range of factors relatively independent of these such as class, age, marital status, fertility patterns, household structure and ideology. The picture that emerges from this study is in many ways an encouraging one in that the factors that have enabled the entry of women into the industrial labour force indicate that the social changes that have taken place in Democratic Yemen have had many positive effects for women. But at the same time a number of problems remain, and these serve to make wage labour especially difficult for women to undertake, thus restricting the participation of women in the labour force and reducing the time they spend in it. These negative influences are, of course, mediated through a variety of different social mechanisms and a full account of their nature and effectiveness is not possible without more detailed research. However, we can indicate some of these mechanisms by referring to the evidence provided by the women workers under two headings: domestic pressures and work restrictions.

3.1   Domestic pressures

We have seen that most women workers in our sample do not as a rule consider marriage in itself as necessarily incompatible with wage work and many of them would like to see themselves continuing to work after marriage. Similarly, most of these women have strong female support structures to help them to overcome the difficulties of combining wage work and domestic responsibility. However, although these women appear to have found some kind of solution to the problem, this does not mean that domestic pressures have ceased to exert a powerful influence over their lives or that they do not constitute a problem. On the contrary although women workers seem to be prepared to postpone marriage and childbearing for a few years while they take up paid employment, postponement can itself be seen as an index of the difficulties of combining wage work with domestic responsibility. Moreover, the solutions women find to their problems are individual, probably short-term, and contingent on a number of factors which cannot be guaranteed over time or indeed to every woman worker. It is obvious from the data that the help women receive from female relatives is conditional on the preservation of strong kin ties, and it would also appear to depend on the maintenance of a certain family size and structure. With the tendency towards smaller families and the valorisation of restricted conjugal units, both by couples themselves and by government housing planners, this matrix of enabling conditions may well be subject to erosion in Democratic Yemen, and with it, the female support structures which facilitate the entry of women workers into industry.

Of the different domestic responsibilities which fall to women, that of child-care appears to be especially problematic in both its subjective and practical aspects. We have noted that child-care was seen by working women as the main problem facing them; in particular, a substantial number of informants expressed anxiety about the effects of their absence from home on their children. As far as the practicalities of child-care are concerned, arrangements are on the whole left for individuals to resolve. There are no nurseries in Democratic Yemen, although a few on-site day-care centres for workers are planned. The provision of kindergartens (for five year olds) is very limited and the hours they are open fall far short of the working day. Working women with children therefore have to find their own solutions; significantly only *one* woman in the sample placed her child in a kindergarten and even she had to rely on her mother to collect him when the school closed.

These individual solutions are not only contingent, but may also cost the working woman a sizeable percentage of her wage packet. In the sample, only one quarter of the respondents kept their wages to themselves. A minority (7.8 per cent) divided it between their husbands and themselves, 31.4 per cent put it in the family kitty and 33.3 per cent divided it between their mothers, other members of the family and themselves. Many of the respondents explained this division of the wage in terms of the payment due for the help they received from their female relatives. If this occurs it reduces the material benefits gained from paid employment and hence the degree of economic independence gained by women workers. This in turn may reduce their stake in remaining in, or participating in, paid employment.

The picture that emerges from this sample is of a young female industrial labour force, relatively unencumbered by domestic responsibilities and relatively interested in continuing to work in the wage economy. Yet, according to factory officials there is a high turnover rate among female workers. Table 36 shows that almost all of the workers (84 per cent) had been in their present place of work for less than three years. The short period of time these women were employed by their enterprise is of course partly accounted for by the fact that some of the factories were only recently established, and by the fact that the workers were themselves for the most part only in their teens and early twenties; none the less, even in the factories with a longer period in production, there still appears to be a high percentage of women with only a year or two of work experience.

The available evidence suggests that despite the existing female support structures, working women are still under considerable pressure to leave work as a result of their domestic responsibilities. The main factor drawing them back into the home is likely to be the care of pre-school children, and it is reasonable to suppose that this too, is a major factor in preventing those women not already in the labour force from entering it. However, although the pressures on women from the domestic sphere are considerable, the reasons why they drop out of the workforce are more likely to be the result of the *interaction* between these domestic pressures and the conditions which prevail on the public, external, front of work. It is to these work conditions that we will now turn.

Table 36: Number of years in present job

No. of years	Absolute no.	%
Less than 1	34	28.3
1	21	17.5
2	42	35.0
3	8	6.7
4	3	2.5
5	7	5.8
6	1	0.8
7	4	3.3
	120	100.0

Source: Author's research.

3.2 Work restrictions

The factors which draw women back into the domestic sphere are complemented by a number of conditions prevailing at work which combine to weaken their commitment to remaining employed. First of all, there is the nature of the work allocated to women; this is often the most tedious and repetitive of the tasks available. Second, there is the lack of promotion prospects attached to these jobs. Third, there is the level of remuneration: the pay for unskilled labour may not be sufficiently attractive to offset the negative aspects of wage work. The small monetary incentives on offer are unlikely to be sufficient compensation for doing a tedious job quickly and well. A factory manager summed up the prevailing view of the problem when he said: "The reason why sewing is women's work is because it is difficult to find a man who will sit for eight hours at a sewing machine. Men cannot tolerate this kind of work. They also dislike it because the wages are low. The fact is that since men are more qualified they can get better jobs with better money."

Of course it is not true that the lower educational level of women accounts on its own for their occupational distribution, nor is it the case that all men are spared from doing jobs which are tedious and badly paid. But planners and factory managers alike work on the basis of these assumptions and see women as especially suited to the more tedious work. Most of those interviewed commended women workers for their patience, and their ability to tolerate work which was admitted to be boring but was none the less demanding. One manager said that women were both more disciplined than men and more amenable to discipline. In his words "they stand still at their work and are obedient". This of course tells us something about the socialisation of women but nothing about whether they enjoy the work they do, or whether they saw it as an important and integral part of their lives.

If the work that women are encouraged to take up is tedious, lacking in promotion prospects and poorly paid, it is even more unlikely that they will develop a clear

78

orientation towards a career or towards any clear goal of promotion to which they might aspire beyond that of supervisor. If there is any question of choice in this situation, the primary pole of attraction may well become the domestic sphere. Here, the difference between men and women unskilled workers is clear; whereas, if material circumstances permit, women have a "place" to return to in the home, men as a rule do not. They are expected either to continue working in their unsatisfying jobs or actively to seek a way out through retraining or saving up to start their own business. Women, however, do not formulate their objectives only in terms of a work orientation; as indicated in the preceding section, they are under strong pressure to retain a fairly strong domestic orientation. Given the rigidity of the sexual division of labour in the home, the presence of small children removes any element of choice for most women; this in turn further disrupts any possibility of advance in employment, and further disadvantages them on the labour market.

The lack of a firm career or employment orientation among women is illustrated most strikingly by the answers respondents gave to the question "what are your main ambitions vis-à-vis your work?" When asked if they had any special ambitions regarding their work, 18.3 per cent replied that they simply wanted to continue to do their job well and had no particular desire for further advancement. Twenty per cent expressed their desire to increase their output and 21.7 per cent wanted to do well at work while continuing their education. Nearly 30 per cent had ambitions outside the realm of work; the most frequently cited aim was to continue their education and make more time available for studying. And 18.3 per cent claimed to have no ambitions regarding their work at all. Despite an expressed desire for self-improvement, what is striking about these responses is that only one person formulated a clear objective in terms of improving her career prospects, in her case through learning to type. This lack of ambition vis-à-vis employment could be a significant factor in causing women to leave their jobs if they see no clear way out of the unskilled or semi-skilled job trap.

The data therefore suggest that the sexual division of labour in industry and at home combine to restrict women's participation in employment both in terms of the numbers of women who come onto the labour market and in terms of the time they spend in employment. While certain changes have taken place to improve the position of women over-all, there remain important differences and inequalities between the sexes through which the position of women is disadvantaged in relation to that of men. In the concluding section we shall consider this problem in more detail and suggest ways in which it might be alleviated.

3. Conclusions

On the basis of this study some initial and tentative conclusions can be drawn. Perhaps the most important general observation to be made is that state intervention and the implementation of a series of radical reforms have done much to improve the position of women in Democratic Yemen and to make it one of the most advanced countries in the Middle East in this regard. Legal reform, the democratisation of education and the encouragement of women to enter employment have eroded some of the worst formal inequalities between the sexes in a relatively short period of time, and have helped to provide the basis for further transformations in the future. Yet each of the gains that have been made requires some qualification. Although women have attained near equality at the formal legal level, they are still far from having realised it in practice; boys and girls have equal rights to education but attendance rates among girls are still low; and while women have attained formal equality in the workplace, sexual asymmetry in the occupational structure still allocates the best jobs to men and many of the worst to women. Government officials recognise these disparities and are hopeful that in time at least some of them will disappear, as the country develops its resources and social and economic development proceeds apace.

Any evaluation of Democratic Yemen's record in the field of women's emancipation has to take two major constraints into account. The first is that this has until very recently been a socially conservative society within which it will take a long time for attitudes to change; legal changes or Party proclamations will not, in themselves, suffice to enable women to attain equality with men. The second constraint is that Democratic Yemen is a poor country unable to devote the necessary material resources to alleviating some of the most basic problems in such areas as pay, nursery facilities, or training schemes. Yet state policy is not just a matter of allocating resources; it also involves establishing priorities and there is reason to believe that, within the constraints identified, some new initiatives could be taken. For more than objective processes and *existing* policies are required if the government is to achieve its expressed aim of sexual equality, and is at the same time to benefit from women's contribution both to the labour force and to society at large. For the government's reforms have so far tended to operate on the public, external front, while in the private, domestic sphere there remain relations and practices which continue to escape the effects of the wider processes, and which at the same time serve to hinder the further advance of women towards equality. Chief among these is the prevalence of a strict sexual division of labour in the home, which allocates to women the main burden of responsibility for housework and child-care. For the working women this constitutes a serious problem for which only short-term and unsatisfactory solutions can be found.

The effects of leaving this area untouched are most strikingly illustrated by the data presented in the preceding analysis of female industrial workers. These women have for the most part received some education and training; they are valued by the state and by their enterprises as experienced and efficient workers who make an important contribution to the economy. They have taken what is, for them, a major step in entering paid employment and they have therefore broken through many of the taboos that still attach to the notion of women working in industry. Yet, they do not remain employed for long and once they have left, it is probable that they will not return.

The reasons why there is a high drop-out rate among women are not hard to find. Because they perform the most tedious jobs with few possibilities, if any, of promotion, they receive little encouragement to develop a longer-term interest in their work. Their wages are not sufficiently attractive and the job not sufficiently interesting for them to value the work particularly highly in itself. In addition, pressures from the domestic sphere make it difficult for women to combine work and home responsibilities. Women everywhere remain vulnerable to "lifecycle" pressures, as their domestic situation at certain key times exercises a determining influence on their employment potential. In particular, women tend to find that the rearing of young children is incompatible with undertaking demanding full-time work; since there has been no redistribution of sex roles within the household in Democratic Yemen, or alleviation of the burden of child-care, women are invariably forced to give up their work when they have young children to care for. They are also given few incentives to return to work after a period of absence. Obviously, major changes are required to overcome this problem and some are beyond the government's limited resources. But it *is* within the government's capacities to alleviate at least some of these difficulties, and to take them into account at the planning stage. On the basis of this research a number of problem areas can be identified.

First, although the existing system of kin-based female support structures serves to assist working women it is not an adequate solution to the problem. It does not tackle the problem of sexual inequality and as a practical solution there is an element of contingency about it. Moreover it may have the effect of keeping women who might otherwise be free to work out of the labour force. In respect of housework the core of the problem is the persistence of sexual inequality. Men do not share equally in the burden of domestic responsibility and do not want to. Attitudes of this kind are strongly entrenched, and although there are some signs of erosion, greater official support needs to be given both to valorise domestic work and to advocate the sharing of it among all members of the household, both male and female. In other words, the privileged relationship that men enjoy in the home must be seen as untenable once women are engaged in wage earning activities. Such ideological changes clearly require the full support of the mass organisations and the educational apparatus as well as of the different organs of the mass communication network.

Second, the whole issue of child-care needs greater consideration. If possible, resources should be made available to establish child-care facilities for pre-school children, with the children of working mothers being given special priority. Since resources are scarce, the feasibility of greater community responsibility could be explored, possibly involving such local political organisations and the Popular Defense Councils and the General Union of Yemeni Women. New housing projects could also ensure that they give priority to the establishment of day-care centres. The possibility of running these, too, on a community basis could be explored. However, as women with young children often prefer to be in close contact with them, the most certain strategy is to make it possible for parents (of either sex) to bring their younger children to work with them. The additional costs of establishing such facilities could well be recovered by reducing the turnover of experienced women workers which in other circumstances almost inevitably result.

Third, a greater effort could be made by the government to encourage those women who do leave the labour force for childbearing purposes to return again after a period of absence. Some kind of incentive system to induce such women to return could be worked out; alternatively, women, and men too, in principle, could under certain circumstances be given a prolonged leave of absence with the right to return to their jobs after two to three years. Special efforts would have to be made to seek out these women and actively encourage their return.

Fourth, some provision needs to be made either on-plant or on a day-release basis, for training those women who are keen to remain in the labour force but who are bored by their work, to retrain or to train up. This would help to alleviate the stifling effects of a too rigid division of labour at the same time as it might stem the flow of women workers out of the labour force.

These measures would, over time, provide the pre-conditions under which women would be better able to participate in the labour force, thus helping the women themselves and simultaneously helping the government to reduce the flow of qualified and experienced women out of the labour force. But, on their own, they may prove inadequate without another transformation of a major kind, viz. the erosion of the sexual division of labour in employment itself. As long as women are channelled into unrewarding occupations with few prospects of advance they are likely to remain less committed members of the workforce. It is only by pursuing a genuine policy of occupational desegregation that those women intent on remaining in paid employment will find it sufficiently rewarding to do so.

The kinds of changes that have been discussed here involve major transformations in the social and economic structure of society, together with transformations in the prevailing ideology. Piecemeal reforms can achieve much, as they undoubtedly have in Democratic Yemen, yet they cannot realise the government's stated objectives of an economically active *and equal* female population. Inherent in government policies are mechanisms and occlusions which unintentionally disadvantage women. The result is that despite all the gains that have been made, progress is slower than it should have been. A poor country is in no position to waste its resources, and measures should be taken to build on the reforms that have so far been implemented. If this does not occur Democratic Yemen may not only be unable to realise one of its constitutional aims, but it may also be unable to benefit from one of its most important assets.

NOTES

1) This seriously affected only a few questions such as household composition which was a very detailed and therefore lengthy response to document and was curtailed because of time constraints.
2) The majority of the women working in factories were in fact under 30 years of age, so this bias should not be exaggerated.
3) The classification skilled/unskilled is increasingly acknowledged to contain an element of arbitrariness and almost invariably works to the detriment of women's work.
4) This can be attributed to the sexual imbalance in Aden during the pre-Independence period.
5) This move away from trade would have been accelerated by the contraction of this sector during the years before and immediately after the revolution.
6) Marriage here means the formal completion of the wedding negotiations and transfer of the bride to the husband's home.
7) This excludes the woman "married" at 3 months.
8) See G. Standing and G. Sheehan (1978) for a clarification of this point.
9) The MCH Report referred to earlier gives the mean number of children (of 1,000 registered) to be 4. Very few of these women were employed.
10) Wikan (1980) reports such a discrepancy between stated preferences and eventual number of children per family.
11) This question could not be included in the questionnaire because of a restriction on the number of questions that could be asked. However, about 25 per cent of the women volunteered that they would like equal numbers of girls and boys, while only about 3 per cent said they would like more sons than daughters. No one said they only wanted sons, but many women did not voice an opinion.
12) The theoretical implications of this for a theory of women's subordination are discussed in Molyneux (1979).
13) This was an open-ended question asking respondents to say if they thought anything had changed since the revolution and if so to say what the main changes were. The answers were classified at a later stage.
14) See Makhlouf (1980) for an account of the position of women of the Yemen Arab Republic and a discussion of the different aspects of veiling (pp. 30–38).
15) A subsample of interviews with students at the University and at the Technical Institute shows little variation with the industrial workers — of the 12 informants five wore the *sheidor* outside the home, five wore neither the *sheidor* nor the veil and two wore both.

BIBLIOGRAPHY

Aden Colony (1955): *Census Report* (Aden, Government Press).

Adenisation Committee (1959): *Report of the Adenisation Committee* (London HMSO).

Beck, L. and Keddie, N. (1979): *Women in the Muslim world* (Chicago, University of Chicago Press).

Bujra, A.S. (1971): *The politics of stratification: A study of political change in a south Arabian town* (Oxford, Oxford University Press).

Democratic Yemen (1975): *The Constitution of the People's Democratic Republic of Yemen* (Aden, Government Press).

Democratic Yemen, Central Planning Commission (1974): *Quinquennial plan for economic and social development, 1974–79* (Aden, Government Press).

Democratic Yemen, Central Statistical Organisation (1973): *Population Census* (Aden, Government Press).

––– (1976): *Education Statistics* (Aden, Government Press).

––– (1977): *Labour Force Bulletin* (Aden, Government Press).

––– (1978): *Industrial Bulletin, 1969–1975* (Aden, Government Press).

Democratic Yemen, Department of Labour and Welfare (1965): *Annual Report* (Aden, Government Press).

Democratic Yemen, General Office for Adult Education and Eradicating Illiteracy (1977): *Taqyim Harakat Mahu al-Ummia wa Ta'alim al-Kebar*, mimeo.

Democratic Yemen, Ketab al-Ahsa al Tarbawi al Sanawi, L-Am (1977): *Annual Education Statistics* (PDRY), mimeo.

Democratic Yemen, MCH Services (1977): *Mother and child health care* (Aden, Government Press).

Democratic Yemen, Ministry of Economy, Commerce and Planning (1968): *Problems facing the emergent state of the People's Republic of South Yemen* (Aden, Government Press).

85

Democratic Yemen, Ministry of Education (1976): *Educational development in the PDRY* (Aden, Government Press).

Education Research Centre (1976): *A field study on girls' education* (Aden, Education Research Centre).

El Saadawi, N. (1979): *The hidden face of Eve: Women in the Arab world* (London, Zed Press).

Engels, F. (1970): "The origin of the family, private property and the State", in *Karl Marx and Frederick Engels Selected Works* (London, Lawrence and Wishart).

General Union of Yemeni Women (1976): *Documents of the GUYW* (Aden, Government Press).

Ghanem, I. (1976): "A note on Law No. 1 concerning the family, People's Democratic Republic of Yemen", in *Arabian Studies*, No. 111, pp. 191–196.

Halliday, F. (1974): *Arabia without sultans* (Harmondsworth, Penguin).

––– (1979): "Yemen's unfinished revolution: Socialism in the south", *Merip Report No. 81*, Vol. 9, No. 8, Oct. (Washington DC).

Ingrams, D. (1970): *A time in Arabia* (London, John Murray).

Jancar, B.W. (1978): *Women under Communism* (Princeton, Princeton University Press).

Lenin, V. (1972): *On the emancipation of women* (Moscow, Progress Publishers).

Makhlouf-Obermeyer, C. (1980): *Changing veils: A study of women in South Arabia* (London, Croom Helm).

Massell, G. (1974): *The surrogate proletariat* (Princeton, Princeton University Press).

Mernissi, F. (1975): *Beyond the veil* (New York, John Wiley).

Molyneux, M. (1979): "Beyond the domestic labour debate", in *New Left Review*, No. 116.

––– (1980): "State policy and the position of women in South Yemen"; in *Peuples Mediterranéens*, No. 12, July/Sept.; also in *Feminist Review*, Vol. 1, No. 1, 1979.

––– (1981): "Socialist countries old and new: Progress towards women's emancipation", in *Feminist Review*, No. 8; also in *World Development*, No. 9/10, 1982.

Standing, G. and Sheehan, G. (1978): *Labour force participation in low income countries* (Geneva, ILO).

Stark, F. (1936): *The southern gates of Arabia* (London, Wiley).

UNFPA (1978): *PDRY: Report of the mission on needs assessment for population assistance*, Report No. 7 (New York, UNFPA).

UN, ECWA (1980): *The population situation in the ECWA region: Democratic Yemen* (Beirut, Population Division ECWA).

Wikan, U. (1980): *Life among the poor in Cairo* (London, Tavistock).

World Bank (1979): *The PDRY: A review of economic and social development* (Washington DC, World Bank).

——— (1980): *Development Report, 1980* (Oxford, Oxford University Press).

——— (1981): *Development Report, 1981* (Oxford, Oxford University Press).

Youssef, N.H. (1973): *Women and work in developing countries*, Population Monograph Series No. 15 (Berkeley, University of California Press).